BRENDA NAKAMOTO

Peach Farmer's Daughter

© 2011 by Roan Press and Brenda Nakamoto · ROANPRESS.COM

Post Office Box 160406, Sacramento CA 95816

ISBN 978-0-9815968-6-0 · first print edition

COLOPHON

body type is Dolly by Bas Jacobs, Akiem Helmling & Sami Kortemäki

header and incidental type is Novel Sans by Christoph Dunst

book design and typeset by Joshua Lurie-Terrell · FLAVORS.ME/JLT

TABLE OF CONTENTS

SUMMER

SONGS OF HARVEST

A line to the past dwindles with each moment,
reincarnated only by reminiscence.
With a crescendo and fading away,
memory drifts in and out like a deep breath.
Sing softly. Sing high and sing low.
Sing, farmer's daughter, from afar.

I was ten years old that summer of over-100-degree weather, hot and humid days with the yeasty smell of peaches ripening behind a dense mat of leaves. I am sure there were many similar summers before, yet for some reason I remember this one as if it were the starting point of memory, of my love affair with farming, of being a farmer's daughter. That is who I am. I sense it, knowing my place, my beginning in time.

When I reflect on farming, I cannot forget the people, those who sweated in the summers or shivered in the winters, tending our orchards and crops. There is this nostalgic rural landscape with rivers and wetlands and cattails and valley oaks. But the people, I do not forget. There were funny men, these peculiar men, in weathered hats and shabby clothes, who magically appeared during harvest. They had dark brown skin. When the geese migrated out of the valley, these men migrated in.

They came seemingly from nowhere—this group with bronzed skin—crammed in sedans with heads and arms dangling from open windows, taking drags on cigarettes and puffing rings of smoke above them. Car after car rambled onto the driveway to our house with engines sputtering and rusty hoods jittering, lighting up a new kind of life. Men lined four across, shoulder to shoulder on vinyl-covered seats, and smiled with yellowed teeth and darkened wrinkles etched above their brows, dirt lines creased in their foreheads.

My mother had not wanted me to socialize with them, the

Mexicans who, with eyes that grinned and unshorn whiskers, squeezed into these rickety cars of faded paint, faces half hidden under frayed sombreros. On the porch, our chubby white Chihuahua snapped and barked while Mom restrained her firmly in her arms. These men laughed, mingling around the cement porch steps, talking with my father, working out details with Jesse the Mexican contractor, who would finalize the labor agreements.

These Mexicans would forever be an enigma to me, seen and not fully understood; Mom said they came from far, down south, from that obscure country called Mexico, where I heard wild dogs roamed and white sandy beaches piled against desolate wilderness for miles. I imagined they came from cactus-covered deserts and small towns with unpaved streets and shanties. These strangers from afar brought unusual presents with them: squares of pungent goat cheese or milk candy with a bitter aftertaste, stacks of chewy tortillas or clay piggy banks molded into the shape of a bull. These were the braceros, the hired men who would pick fruit from our orchards. Dad needed them for the harvest; they needed us for our money. It must have been an even exchange, this joining of business and culture, done with a mere shaking of hands between Jesse and my dad and uncle. That Mom and Dad grumbled later behind Jesse's back about his nickel-and-diming a commission from the men for everything—for every bin picked, every hour worked—didn't change things. Now we were all bonded to each other, our lives conjoined, and for me, it was like I had instantly gained a whole bunch of brothers.

Part of a fifty-man crew, some of the new hires moved onto our ranch into the makeshift space that would be their home for the season. Long before their arrival, Dad and I had prepared their living quarters from the area where the farm equipment had been repaired and stored, where a roof of nailed aluminum sheets sheltered tractors and implements from inclement weather. During summers when the men

came, Dad emptied this part of our farming shed and transformed it into what looked to me like a military barracks.
Silver-grey planks of wood paneled the outer walls, and a three-
foot-wide swath of metal screening for windows ran across
one end to the other. There was no form of air conditioning.

We unlocked the plywood box with rusty hinges that creaked
a staccato tune when pulled open; and we grappled with the
stack of thin mattresses inside, placing them in double piles
on the cement floor on top of each other, where they hugged
tightly like mating ladybugs. Metal and wire bunk beds lined
single file down this long and narrow corridor, set apart from
the main area of the tool shed.

A solitary light bulb dangled from above, portions of the electrical wire exposed to open air. *Clickity click.* A jerk on a worn
and rusted chain turned on the incandescent light that softly
illuminated the dust-filled darkness as it swung. A wide push
broom whisked across the floor, sweeping a ridge of dirt and
debris before it. Then Dad appeared from behind the cloud
of dust, brown shirt and pants matching the earth tones of
his occupation. He was a chameleon, meant to be a farmer,
stepping in and out of shadow, dusting off the year's worth of
debris accumulated in that shed. Then he was gone, sitting on
the leather seat of a humming tractor, fired up and ready to
take him to the next task.

I didn't mind the dust airborne and fluttering around me.
Here, one was close to the earth. We were together breathing
with the soil, touching the loam crumbling and breaking in
our fingertips. It was the life we all knew. It was what sustained
our farm, our families, and the hungry people at the market.
It was the soil that imparted energy to our lives. We farmers
and braceros who labored—sowing seeds and tending branches—filled our hands with the fruits of harvest because of
this earth. And when all was said and done—the farmers' and
braceros' final toils in the fields—this soil would still be here
long after our departure.

We had scrubbed the bathroom, a separate building of cinder block my father had constructed, filled with three shower heads mounted in a line behind a dividing cement wall and one urinal, two toilets and a sink. High above and just under the ceiling, leggy spiders strung wispy webs across chunky wooden beams where narrow slats of sky peeked from above. Underground, squirrels tunneled below the concrete slab, familiar with the noise of human traffic. Long before I neared them, they scampered into their burrows, dragging and flicking wiry tails. Many creatures shared these rural quarters, confirming in yet another way how we were joined together. The world of the peach farm was my daddy's business, yet it was more than that. It was my world: my trees, my animals, my trucks and tractors.

How could the farm and these men have touched me so? Decades later, they are still there in my dreams, lurking under the salt of summer sun, with sultry breaths and toothpicks in moist lips, carrying splintery ladders and canvas bags. And the dog barked, and we children whooped and hollered while Mom and Auntie Chi sorted through the waist-high bins of peaches, pushing undersized fruit lying on top through circular sizing rings.

That the men looked different from us and spoke differently didn't matter much to me. My eyes followed their movements in the field, up and down ladders like spiders weaving webs and rappelling. There was this ominous monotony enmeshed in the drone of the distant tractor engine with each hour that passed during those seemingly endless days. I listened; I heard snappy tunes and voices intermixed with the creaks and groans of the wooden bins being lifted and transported from tree to tree. They chattered, these fifty men, with the banter of resounding hellos and curses exchanged amongst each other across the field while they picked pink and orange and yellow balls of sweet fruit off branches.

The hot afternoon lifted dust around my footprints, and I had walked close to the bend in the road where the camp met the border of disked soil and asphalt driveway, where a building jutted out toward the orchard. Having finished picking peaches for the day, the men were preparing their dinner. It was late, in the hottest period of summer, and I could hear recorded music, the lilting tenor and bass passages of Spanish songs filled with lyrics I could not understand. I didn't need to know the meaning of the foreign words, because I could feel the nuances of their language in voices that tugged at me.

They liked the lighthearted, whimsical rancherias. Sometimes a man bellowed and hollered, matching the giddy yips and yells that floated out of scratchy radio speakers from inside a darkened kitchen, amidst the abrupt aroma of chile and cumin and the clank and clatter of water spraying against pots and pans. It was a room painted in olive drab, like fatigues, with an industrial-size stainless steel sink and a blackened, sooty gas stove placed next to a refrigerator and a picnic bench. I peeked inside the doorway through the narrow slant of space propped open by a chair. I knew my mom wouldn't want me to be here, so close to all these foreign men. She'd say I shouldn't watch them, that it was wrong. Wrong like the boy who chased me across the playground at school. I ran, I screamed. Same thing. We were afraid of eye contact, wary of the touch of a hand, even the suppressed smile in a furtive look. We must not reveal too much of ourselves to others. Be always careful, quiet. From the corner of my eye, I watched the men, I observed them, standing casually or lounging on chairs without their shirts, brown skin glistening in sweat from that hot afternoon. I looked despite my mother's restrictions; there was no way I could not notice.

Occasionally, I had good reason to visit the men in the camp. Having picked three cooking pots full of vegetables from our garden, Mom suggested I take a bag to the Mexicans.

"Give it to the men," she would say, unloading the biggest, fattest zucchini and cucumbers and chunky green beans into a paper grocery bag. I didn't question. After all, it was like we had a whole city block in our backyard, and I knew nothing about my neighbors.

I walked towards their camp, my scrawny arms around the bulging bag, taking steps in inch-deep dust that meant my sneakers would never be completely clean again. I approached, past the two empty oil barrels that served as trash cans, past a large circular metal plate from a disk harrow that hung above the kitchen doorway, thanks to my father. Perhaps that was a gong, a dinner bell or doorbell. I never used it; no one ever did. It hung silent.

From around the building, I heard foreign voices reciting mysterious sounding incantations. What were they saying? See that little girl walking towards us? Like a mouse! What a funny thing! The voices laughed and grunted in jocular intonations. Then the chatter stopped as they looked at me.

Some sat on rickety wooden chairs in the shade outside the kitchen. Others stood upright, leaning against the wall. Many were dark and tanned, sporting fresh-shaved moustaches clipped neatly to their lips. A shadowy figure moved from behind a window screen; I heard the fizzle, crackle and pop of food bubbling in oil. The men recognized me and nodded and waved. I felt awkward. I didn't even know most of their names.

One man got up and off his seat to greet me. That was Carmen, one whom I could recognize. He was like a grandpa, wearing a battered straw fedora, his skin the stain and texture of seasoned leather. But he was soft inside, past the mouth with missing and crooked teeth, past the lungs that heaved in that summer heat; he was warm and caring and honest. He was like a buffalo nickel—you can't find many like them anymore.

I volunteered in broken Spanish the little I had learned in

school. "Hola," I started to say. I couldn't say much more. Maybe I'd add a "¿Cómo estas?," but then I wouldn't know what to say if anyone answered. It's best in times like this to simply raise a fattened, foot-long cucumber in one's hands. Carmen's eyes sparkled. How embarrassing for me with this cucumber. It was a big and tough one my mother didn't want.

"Gracias," he said and he unburdened the paper bag from my hands. I felt naked with nothing to hide behind. I smiled back, a big cheesy grin as my dimples burst from my cheeks and I crossed my clumsy feet. One of the others picked from the bag, wiped the vegetable on his pants, brushing off the dirt and spikes, then sank his teeth into flesh. In this fresh gouge, pearl-like seeds of the fat cucumber gleamed. The sun laughed from above and I was delighted. This was just the kind of thing I would do.

The braceros whistled and sang while they worked during the day picking peaches, they whistled and sang while preparing their meals, and they whistled and sang with the sun slumbering, after having showered and when relaxing on top of the packed dirt. It was time for bed. All was dark; the air was still and unbearably stifling. One could have not a strip of clothing on, be lying on top of sheets and not able to sleep because the night was as heavy as a sauna, sucking moisture from my insides and layering it on my skin. Misery.

Not a hint of wind moved. Lying in my own damp ring of sweat, I swatted at kamikaze mosquitoes that buzzed by my ears. They were an insomniac's nightmare. I would look up through the open window, at the moon and stars rich and bright across the sky, and I would imagine places elsewhere—the dark, inviting recesses of blackness sprinkled in the Milky Way. I was so very little; this universe was so very big.

I thought of the men sweltering in the camp. Did the Mexicans dream, too? Sounds drifted from across the yard, interspersed with another occasional whistle. Such harmony! They filled the hollows of space between my thoughts. For a moment, the clear, crisp tone of a serenade from a tenor voice reached out to me lying in bed, across the roadway separating myself from the men.

I listened closely—to a sound of harmony—and it was like the moon shifted, the veil of grey night parted; and I wondered if he was singing to someone waiting for him hundreds of miles away, for certainly these men had women: their mothers, their girlfriends, wives or children. That lonely tremor, sonorous and desolate, cleaving the melancholy night, illuminated the disparities between us and the beauty we both shared.

These men led a life quite different than mine, theirs following the seasons, drifting with the ripening of crops in a land foreign, living far away from familiarity. I think of Carmen and his son Alfredo. Whatever happened to them? They worked with us for two summers and then never returned. I hope they have done well and prospered. Perhaps they have wondered about me as I wonder about them now.

Sing again. Sing with them, farmer's daughter.

For me there could be no better childhood: the pitch-black mornings at the start of harvest; the wicked heat of the noontime summer sun; the evening's tenacious mosquitoes; and the windless, humid nights. I loved that farm and the men. Even years later, their music will never escape me.

the Nakamotos harvesting peaches

BRENDA NAKAMOTO

LISTENING TO HARVEST

Some peaches fall naturally from orchard trees long before having a chance to be harvested. Fruits high in a canopy exposed to scorching summer sun ripen into orange rumps amongst the foliage, earlier than those hidden in the shadows below. They smell candy sweet, the overripe ones a bit sour. A gentle wind jostles the branches, bark bending and swaying, and fruits hanging from woody umbilical cords to mother trees are loosening their grips.

Thug-splot...

Peaches in various stages of decomposition litter the ground as submerged ovals floating in an earthen sea of mud, with half of their mummy husks poking up in mushroom-like heads clustering the trunks of trees. Stand quietly in the orchard forest long enough and quietly enough and you will hear the peaches dropping.

Thug-splot...

They drop and plunge in one graceful motion, gravity pulling them downward from the safety of high branches to the earth below. Dotting the orchard floor and splattered in the soil, some might still be suitable for human consumption, if rescued immediately. But the clay and its ecosystem of predators attack the vulnerable fruit; fallen peaches expire quickly and decay from sugars to starches and then into moldy spheres of furry rot. Once plucked from the tree, the shelf life of a fresh peach is fleeting. It is now a race for the farmer to get the fruit to market, like my daddy who raises these peaches to feed someone in this world, someone he won't ever knowingly see or touch, someone who will not even think of him when opening a can of processed cling peaches purchased at the market. But that doesn't matter at this moment.

We are hoping to defy the odds, to fight decay; it is our life's savings on the line, resting here within these branches. The year's unpaid bills beckon.

The sound and sight of falling peaches unnerved my father. For every peach that fell, he counted money lost, because each tree with fruit was an investment. In some ways, these trees were like us children. Dad felt responsible for them. They made him who he was out of necessity. Caring for the trees year-round, he shepherded them like a flock—pruning, spraying, thinning, irrigating—always absorbed in chores. He bore these tasks and burdens as if fathering tens of thousands of children and rearing them through adulthood. He thinks only of getting the ripened peaches picked and into the bins for the cannery, so that he can haul them down the road to the grading and receiving station where the semitrucks await.

Thug-splot... Peaches are falling.

My father cursed and swore. He had miscalculated. Irrigating the trees one last time before picking, he pumped a layer of well water onto the floor of the orchard, wetting the Carolyns, a variety soon to be picked with its glowing crop of fruit. Any good peach farmer would do this, expecting to fatten up the peaches with one last drink. Good size meant higher tonnage. Increased tonnage meant more money, and he needed that, oh, how we all needed that money. The water coincidentally ran at the same time a heat wave tumbled into the valley, temperatures suddenly driving the mercury in thermometers well over the 100-degree mark, blushing the peaches scarlet. Now there wasn't time to stop the irrigation water; there wasn't time to let the wet soil dry. It was too late. The soil softened to gooey clay, sticky as putty, and machinery couldn't get in, nothing could get in: no pickers, no forklifts, no trucks. Only my mother and father and me, walking in muddy boots between tree rows. We are losing the ripe ones.

BRENDA NAKAMOTO

Peaches fall into the mud never to be picked by a human hand, never touched or fondled. We'd have to wait for the ground to dry, for it to harden and bear weight again. Otherwise, wheels will only spin and machinery will wallow in muck. There is almost nothing worse than watching the entire crop of peaches hanging on the branches, turning from a shade of light green to yellow-red and then the overripe of pumpkin orange and not be able to do a darn thing about it. What a curse. We halt the pickers and wait in silence, sitting at the dining room table and thinking about the drooping branches of the Carolyns, flushed with fruit.

Hold on tight, peaches, don't worry. We're going to get you. Daddy's coming.

Some sounds, even the *thug-splots* of the world, can be sometimes better than the absence of sound—silence. Silence tossed in with rolling mist. Silence when the farm animals are pacing and anxious. Quiet, like something lurking, the dog sniffing the air and bristling the hair on his neck as he paws the earth and yelps at the sky. The air thickens; clouds congeal, jelling into a soupy mass. The threatening sky tumbles into the valley amidst the angst of farmers who are banking-out their crops from the fields.

The air heavy with moisture, suffocating like a damp towel, suffuses the orchard in grey. Grey like old dishwater, grey from weeping, grey with clouds jogging low along the skyline.

The air hangs thick, the bosom of the clouds caressed by the peach treetops, the leafy canopy infatuated and brushing close. The tropical storm, full of a holiday spirit in the middle of August, laughs and burps into the valley, pushing aggressively over the Coast Range, splaying over the valley floor.

I watch the rolling cloud wisps churn above me. We had been hearing about her arrival—this tropical storm aroused to the west—and we farmers had been glued to the television and radio reports. Don't come, we say. She came. In the dead of summer with the harvest in full swing, nothing except frantically taking out the produce from field to processing plant could calm our nerves. We had worked long and hard for many days, but there is only so much one can do, only a certain pace at which peaches can be picked with what resources we had. The storm clouds somersault, despite my prayers to the rain gods asking to stay what may be unleashed. If dances could be performed supplicating a momentary reprieve, I would have danced in a ritual. Anything would help. Dear rain gods, please hear me.

A lone raindrop hits my cheek, carried by the crackle and rumble of thunder skipping across the ground and careening away. Another drop falls; more and more fall. Then soon the orchard trees, once silent in the humid, still air, suddenly chorus in unison, as raindrops coalesce into rivulets and sheets driven by gusts. The trees sigh in repose, tepid water rushing down their leaves. What do they know? Their fruits will rot, consumed by fungus. Do not relax in this sultry shower. It is mere deception.

Stay these tears. Don't cry. This foreboding hangs above me, not to be pushed away, not to be blown out of the horizon with a friendly puff of dry wind from the north. The storm waits, knows we cannot escape.

"What now, honey?" I hear my mother's voice. "It's quitting time!" Dad shouts. My Uncle Bob whistles a short, shrill call above the roar of the storm. "¡Nada mas trabajo, no más, no más!" [No more work, no more, no more!] "¡Andele!" [Hurry!] "Stack up the ladders! Tractors to the house! Haul in the bins!"

People scurry in the rain, backs hunched and hat brims angled down below eyebrows, rain drizzling off the edges like skating, running gutter water. Voices uttering Spanish fly chaotic across the field. The Mexican workers arrange quickly their ladders into a pile and disappear. The sputtering hiccups of their car engines fade as the last of them vacates our farm. Then there is only the falling rain with my father and me who are inside the overhang of the shed where the tractors and truck and a few bins of picked fruit are drying underneath. The rain gushes outside, sheeting off the edges of the roof in a waterfall. The patter of raindrops on a hundred panels of corrugated aluminum thunders above us.

The storm drums downward in syncopated bursts.

Tomorrow. We can always hope for tomorrow.

Suyeno Nakamoto (Baachan)
irrigating field crops

WATER

I splash in water, sandy mud oozing between my toes. A short distance away, boiling and snowy white, pumped groundwater plunges from the foot-wide irrigation pipe and froths through a narrow sluice of cement before settling into a wide flat of shallows, where I am wading underneath the peach limbs. The translucent liquid runs smooth and silky over my feet in this artificial current, and the muddied bottom stirred up by my toes settles down and clears: water polishing the silt and sand and making them shine like diamonds. There's gold underneath, and every pinprick sparkle of yellow lures me to plunge my hands into the icy cold and collect bits of iron pyrite on my palms. Out of the artificial stream and drying quickly in my hands, the polished rocks never look quite as alluring, because water changes things.

I am frolicking in my own personal river less than a foot deep. Opaque and iridescent, the cellophane-wrap surface of water beyond the rapids near the irrigation pump runs smooth and mirrored, perfect for a leisurely float on an inner tube, legs and arms out like a crab, or on one's back, stiff as a board. The trick is to keep one's buttocks up and off the silt bottom. Otherwise, shorts and panties soon fill up with sand, and then it's like sandpaper scraping away skin. When you're all done and later cleaning up in the shower, a pile of rocks sprinkles the tub floor.

Cousins Rod and Glen and I take turns splashing in the narrow irrigation ditch, and we squeal and cry out in laughter on our bumper car rides in inner tubes, gnashing and bouncing against one another. Dry summer air blows on our faces while our toes wrinkle, the pads of our feet changing to a ghostly white. We relish this water; it sustains our life. Summer in this valley is just too darn hot. And Rod, Glen and I, yelping like puppies and playful as kittens, contort our faces, tussling, sloshing and horsing around.

Water fills the spaces between the meandering two-foot-high levees. Ridges of soil slink between watery reflections of morning sun, and this farmscape transforms into a checkerboard sequence of dry soil, irrigated marshy soil, and then mud. Water migrates from one portion of the landscape to the other; it leapfrogs across the orchard. It moves due to a rarely seen force—my father.

Daddy approaches the water in hip waders and balances a shovel on his shoulder, one hand on the wooden handle and the other held out for balance when he trudges through the foot-deep mixture of mud and water. Leaves and sticks and bugs float on top of this temporary swamp, and the surface of this mucky goo hugs close to the top of one check. One side of the ridge is saturated in water, the other dry and ready for a cut. It has taken hours for this one to fill. He navigates the ribbons of elevated dirt dividing one section from the next, where only a thin line of dry soil remains on the surface. He arrives to a spot marked with fluorescent paint on a peach tree trunk and digs swiftly with his shovel into the nearby ridge. A small sliver of water escapes its confines, and soon more water and leaves and debris stream outward, carving deep into the ridge as momentum widens the break. This we call "cutting" a check.

When the irrigation water runs, Daddy hardly sleeps, because it's a twenty-four-hour, round-the-clock job to irrigate from one side of the orchard to the other. Checks fill, get cut, then drain, fill, get cut, then drain. He catnaps throughout the nights, keeping his waders and clothes next to the laundry room door for easy exit and reentry. He sometimes takes us daughters with him.

My sister Arlene recalls going into the almond orchard with the moon full and bright. She reminisces: "The stars were twinkling, and the air was clear and warm. We had to wait for the check to fill, so we laid against the ridge looking at the stars and moon and listening to the flowing water. It was a

BRENDA NAKAMOTO

very peaceful moment and I remember thinking what a beautiful life we had. The moment ended when, as quick as quick could be, on Dad's command, we were in action with shovels cutting the check."

We take for granted what we once had. We take for granted things as simple as water flowing along the earth's surface.

Water slips through my hands, drips off my fingertips; it is almost invisible. Then it evaporates and no one will remember: not the trees, not the person in the car speeding by on the county road, not even the postal worker who drops mail in the mailbox. Once, there had been water flowing through the orchard that nourished the crops, the deluge my father had created, and the floating sea of life between the spaces.

O SHO TTO

"O sho tto!" my mom says. She uses this phrase to give her-self power, to give us power. We grunt and shove: Uncle Bob, Auntie Chi, my mom, my cousins and me. We are pushing the old jalopy, stuck in mud with its tires spinning. Dad is in the open cab of the stripped-down pickup truck converted to a dune buggy, foot pressing the gas pedal to the floor, engine shrieking, back wheels shimmying.

He curses, "Dammit!" The jalopy rocks, the back tires splatter-ing soil out of the widening holes coated tumultuously with a film of polished mud. Then, slowing, spinning wheels ease back into the ruts.

Again, gas pedal presses fully down. Engine screeches, jalopy jumps. Rockabye baby. This time jalopy swings forward, then back, oil pan skimming the earth, fender and tailpipe scrap-ing ragged indentations into the topsoil. Keep steady pressure. Watch your feet.

"O sho tto!" We shove our hands on the sides of the frame, some of us next to those slimy, spinning wheels, while others of us grimace just behind the bumper, catching sprays of mud and dirt flung onto our faces. The half-submerged jalopy tires peek out of a rut, ready to jump, then relax and slump back.

"Dammit!" Dad repeats. He can never give up. He stomps again his foot on the gas pedal and the engine roars to life, the frame shivering under our hands.

Mom can't push much harder. After a hysterectomy, she'd never fully regained her strength. Yet she is there with the rest of us, wrapped in one of Daddy's old long-sleeve, plaid shirts, a straw hat with a yellow ribbon tied to her head, heaving her shoulder onto the jalopy with all her might.

My, what fun! I glance at cousins Rod, Dennis, and Glen beside me, gloved hands clenched with mine on the welded iron and plywood. We kids dare not even giggle.

"O sho tto!" We lean once again. Insolent machine!

Something gives, finally. You can hear it in the sound of the engine, a clear, crisp calling of power when we feel the vehicle lurch forward, and we sense it is the jalopy winning. It is us winning. Spinning rear wheels inch forward, out of their confining earthen prisons. Mud-slathered rubber tires crawl up and onto the level surface of orchard floor. We who are pushing fall forward; there is now little resistance. Dad lets up on the gas, the engine stalls, and the jalopy jerks to a sudden stop. Then all is quiet except for the sound of our breathing.

BRENDA NAKAMOTO

THAT WAS WAY COOL

Rod, Glen, and I stand on the deck of a one-lane wooden bridge bolstered atop cement supports. Underneath us flows irrigation water more than ten feet deep, dark green and brown and carrying a load of fine river sediment. The Feather River shares a part of itself by way of these canals, supplying water that traverses miles from the main tributary to thirsty valley crops inland. Grasses and perennials buffer the edges of the mud-lined banks that contain this manmade flow. Water meets land in a narrow strip of shallows, where minnows dart and water striders skate atop a surface occasionally marred by bits of translucent aquatic grasses. This water smells of marsh, dank and ripe with life. The day is calm, quiet and hot; I like it.

Earlier, we had all floated on inner tubes in this canal. Time and again throughout our long and hot summer vacations, we looked to this river water to provide relief. We yelled, "Banzai!" and jumped into the water with ripped denim shorts, T-shirts and tennis shoes. Shoes protected our feet from hitting broken bottles or cans that dotted the channel below the water line. There were few access points to the canal without going through thickets of blackberry brambles or poison oak lining the water's edges. Splash! We hung on the inner tubes and treaded water as the pulse of energy from the river pushed us downstream. On a typical hundred-plus-degree day, these dips were a wonderful diversion. A bridge loomed ahead. This was where the county road crossed from one side to the other. Depending on how much water the farmers were drawing from the canal for crop irrigation, the height of the water beneath the bridge could vary from one foot to three feet. This time the water was pretty high, and we were looking at a breathing space of about one foot. I had never swum under the bridge with such a narrow margin before. We looked at our approaching obstacle. The thought crossed my mind of drowning. There were reports every summer in the local newspaper of lives lost in the canals and river. People dove into the murky waters and hit things hidden beneath. Sometimes there was alcohol involved; sometimes it was just bad luck. Well, we weren't diving off the bridge; we were going under it. And there was probably nothing hidden underneath—I hoped. A picture of abandoned tires and submerged trees flashed momentarily in my mind.

"Come on, let's do it. Are you chicken?" Rod taunted.

Yes I am. It's too late.

The bridge drew nearer, ten feet, six feet, three feet, two feet. We were passing the first cement reinforced girder that spanned the side. The water didn't give us much breathing room. We tilted our heads in a back float position so our faces were flat with the water and we looked straight up. Darkness. From bright light to sudden absence, our eyes at first could see only blurs. Spider webs dangled from wooden planks running crosswise between the girders. Yikes, I hoped there were no black widows here. I didn't want them jumping on my face. The noise of nesting swallows deafened our ears. They chattered angrily. Some of the adults flitted above us, swooping and diving as we floated by. Nests of meticulously dabbed mud covered with feathers and feces clustered the beams. Tiny, downy heads popped up at the edges of the little clay structures, looking at us. We were under the narrow bridge for only a few seconds, then we were propelled back in the bright sunlight when we swam to the bank of the canal and pulled ourselves out of the water. I was relieved. In a moment, with my fears forgotten, I boasted, "That was fun!"

That tubing adventure repeated numerous times since engrained a certain kind of confidence, enough so that the next kind of new activity we could dream of seemed always but a moment away. So when we three are, again, on top of that wooden bridge, we quickly grasp the wooden beams of a short fence-like structure with our hands, swing over our legs, bend our knees and clamber atop the whitewashed railing, giving us a good five feet of distance between us and the water's surface. The beams are husky and thick as railroad ties; these are barricades of the bridge that prevent cars from spilling over, probably meant also for kids like us, but we don't care.

Scratched inscriptions mar the splintery wood, dried out and weathered from years of sun, frosts, and rain. Engraved with deep cuts are those who have visited before: Mark loves Mary. Susan and Steve. JT + CB. True love. We whittle parts of ourselves into this landscape; we leave reminders. I rub my fingertips on the indentations and wonder what this person might have looked like, how old they had been. Were they grown up now? We hope someone will remember us, those whom we loved, maybe those who had even hurt us. I scrape my feet on the white paint and kick off shriveled white flakes into the current of the water below me. I stand on the bridge beam, my outstretched arms maintaining delicate balance. I watch the water skirt underneath.

"Come on!" Rod yells. He signals to jump then launches himself off the railing, closing his eyes and plugging his nose with his fingers. I follow. On that scorching hot, summer day, with an overhead noontime sun looking down upon us, we fling ourselves feet first into cool river water. It's a bit shocking at first. A misty darkness engulfs me, this inviting murky medium. It is different than the chlorinated city pool that's clear blue and stings your eyes if you swim in it too long; I sense this water that I jump into is alive. It pulses with energy. It has power. The initial momentum from the jump propels me deep below. I hold my breath. Then a few swift kicks of my feet pop me toward the yellow sunlight filtering through a brown, glassy haze. I pull with my arms. My head breaks above the surface, and I am already far from where I had jumped. I hear the rush of water spilling over the boards of the weir downstream that form a dam across the levee banks.

I arch my arms in quick strokes slanting me forward and diagonal across the current, I swim hard, inching towards the edge where I can overcome the strength of the pulsing water. I grab onto the circular handle of the irrigation intake valve that diverts water into the neighboring farmer's field. The gate is closed, and I hoist first my legs and then my chest onto a narrow slab of cement just underneath and to the side of the bridge. I stand up and shake off the dripping water. It feels good.

Glen follows us and we three take turns jumping. Then, Rod gets a crazy idea, and he eyes the pile of rocks on the dry side of the levee used to help brace the soil. Walking monkey style, hands swinging between his legs, he hauls a foot-round boulder to where we are on the bridge. He finds a loose strand of twine Dad and Uncle Bob use to tie up the peach tree branches and starts wrapping it about the rock.

"You really want to do what?" I repeat. "I mean—I don't know what you expect to find down there." Rod wants to see what's at the bottom of the canal.

He nods. That's my cousin, full of curiosity and spirit and wanting to learn what makes things tick. He says when he grows up he's going to be a veterinarian or a biologist. He loves animals. "Go ahead," I say even though I think otherwise. Sweat runs down our faces as we work atop that frying pan of a bridge. I like being slippery with sweat; I like feeling the burning rays of sun on my face. I creep down to the edge of the cement slab and splash water on my neck and head. Rod loops the twine several times over the boulder, ties it firmly with multiple knots. He pulls taut the string, hanging the boulder off the ground. Everything holds.

He says, "Ah, come on. Go in with me. All I'm gonna do is hold onto it and let it sink. I just want to see what's down there. There's gotta be a lot of fish, then I'm coming right up."

Rod tugs a toy snorkel mask over his eyes, takes it off, steps to the side of the grassy bank and dips it into the brown-green river water drifting at a fast clip. He snaps the elastic band over the back of his head, pushes down the soft rubber on his face and hears the faint hiss of suction pulling his skin.

"That's better," he says.

Rod glances at me through the scratched plastic lens. I look back, not saying a word.

Should I? Umm...really, there was no way I was getting into that water with him, though the thought of jumping in for a momentary cool down crosses my mind. I don't need to think very long. As much as I want to hang with my cousin, as tomboy as I think I am, certain factors always seem to divide us.

I am a scaredy cat. It's that simple.

"No," I say.

I look at Rod, watch what he's doing, note how intently he goes about his business. Rod can deftly skip rocks multiple times across the water, can drag and carry the heaviest branches across the orchard as well as any of the grown-ups can. He and Glen can swing hammers, drive in nails, spin and whirl wrenches and sockets, hunt pheasants and ducks with shotguns; and what can I do? I sew aprons and bake cookies. I can make a mean summer fruit punch that I pour in frosted glasses and carry out to my dad and uncle working on machinery in the shed. Yes, I am good at some things.

So I look at Rod and watch what he is doing, hear how he commands his younger brother.

"Glen," he says, "when I get under the bridge and into the water, I want you to lower the rock until I grab it. Then when I say so, let go."

Glen nods. He's the quiet brother, probably because being the youngest sibling, like me, makes one more observant watching the antics of older kids. We young ones are no dummies. Glen obeys. Skinny as a string bean, short and compact, he positions himself at the edge of the bridge, slowly lowering the rock over the whitewashed railings until it skims the surface of the canal water.

"Hey, can I do it after you?" Glen asks.

"Of course not, you're too little," Rod answers.

That was close to the truth. However, had we thought a bit more about it, we might have figured my Auntie Chi, if she had known, would have certainly yelled at us. Rod and I were hardly older or for that matter, much bigger than Glen.

"Ready, Glen?" Rod asks, standing on a short cement embankment just under and to the edge of the bridge.

"Aye, aye, captain, preparing for the dive!" Glen musters in a deepened and squeaky voice.

I watch Glen lower the boulder off the side, letting a line of twine lengthen over the whitewashed wooden railing.

"Ready," Glen repeats. The boulder sways a few inches over the water's surface.

"Five ... four ... three ... two ... one," Rod counts. He draws his arms over his head. From the side and underneath the bridge, he dives into the canal, his shirtless bronzed skin skimming the water, then submerging under white froth with his kicking legs. He surfaces and swims, angling diagonal and upstream. Within moments he has reached the hanging boulder. He grabs and tugs.

"Got it," he calls. "Let it go."

Then Glen lets out slack and Rod and the rock disappear into the water's depths with hardly more fanfare than the sound of a single plop. I watch air bubbles rise to the surface until the last of them break and disappear and there is nothing to see except the twine slanting upward and into Glen's hands, angling against the water.

Moments pass. It is now only Glen and me on the deck of the bridge, our forearms resting against the wood, our heads tipped down, anxiously scanning the water's slick facade where Rod had been. The sound of canal water rushing over the wooden boards of the weir thirty yards downstream torments our wait. But I am not worried; of course not.

As if answering my thoughts, within moments Rod pops his head out of the water right next to the line and looks up at us on the bridge smiling and laughing through his water-filled mask. "That was way cool!" he shouts, and again gliding with fluid strokes, he kicks and thrashes across the canal back to the cement slab, where he gets out. Water streams off his hair. He shakes it in wet-doggie fashion before slicking it back out of his face with his hand. He steps off the cement, climbs to the top of the bank through the blackberry brambles and approaches us, jean shorts saturated and dripping. "There were tons of fish down there. I could see them! They're just hanging out."

I wonder how he could have seen anything in all that river muck. Though, if anyone could, it would certainly be Rod.

"How could you tell?" I ask.

"They were right there, all around me!" Rod gives me a discriminating look.

And then I wish I had gone with him. I want to hang with everything he can do. I don't want to be scared, no, of course not. I could have been down there, within a hand's grasp of the long whiskers of the catfish or a bony carp.

Then again, maybe it's better this way—to look at Rod, to see his face glowing and cheeks bursting, to hear him boasting. He is strong and maybe I am not as strong. Yet, certainly, it is a pleasure to experience feelings as I look through his eyes, to be with him in these moments of victory.

SUMMER HARVEST

As I was growing up on the peach farm in the 1970s, harvesting peaches changed completely, with the invention, manufacturing, and introduction of mechanized harvesters. Two massive machines on wheels, combined with hydraulics, conveyor belts and horsepower, all but replaced the crews of fifty men my father normally hired for picking our orchards in the summers. With my father's and my uncle's combined families of ten people and two new machines, we could handle almost the entirety of the harvest alone. In that way, we were more in control of the tenuous peach picking process. This method, however, did have its drawbacks: fruit damage, tree scarring, the frequent need to replace older trees, dependence on fossil fuels, and the vehicular maintenance that went along with it. If a machine broke down, the entire harvest halted. My family retired from the farming industry in 1985. Subsequently, after some years of accepting farmers' bruised peaches, the canneries changed their policies and eventually discouraged processing mechanically harvested fruit. I have heard that most of the peach growers in our region have reverted to the traditional hand-picking method.

The shaker, atop four wide tires with Uncle Bob at the steering wheel, crawls up to a peach tree and extends a mechanical arm about the base of the trunk. With slanted bars of steel armor above, sloping at an angle and coated with cushioned, black padding, my uncle's vehicle awaits its other half.

Driving the catch frame is his son, my cousin Rodney. Standing behind him is his mom—my auntie Chi—and me on the opposite side, sorting on a platform. A four-foot-square wooden bin hangs from the rear on giant forks that lower and elevate it off the ground. My mother walks beside it on the orchard floor, waiting.

Rodney maneuvers his machine, creeps at an angle towards the clutched tree, the front and back wheels controlled with independent steering. He carefully positions the catch frame next to the main trunk. With hydraulics he lowers the fruit-receiving receptacle running the length of over twenty feet, exposing a long and narrow gully that fits snugly with the shaker arm. It meets the ground with a thud. The shaker now lowers a portion of its slanted pads and the lone nadir peach tree surrounded by machines awaits its offloading, encapsulated completely by steel slats and rubber padding.

I had been riding on the catch frame for hours, in and out of scorching sun and dappled shade. Tree after tree. How many had we finished and how long had we been out here—sweat soaking long sleeves and pants, breathing clammy air under dust masks, wet and soggy from expiry? Unbearably long. I lick my lips and taste salt. I feel the pin pricks of peach fuzz bunched in skin folds on my neck and arms.

"Don't scratch," my mother has said, "it makes it worse."

I try to think of other things, anything, but this darn itch. The conveyor belt squeaks. Peaches ride from below to above, atop the train of slots of the conveyor belt. They dump onto a chain link belt where we are positioned at the back of the catch frame. A river of fruit runs before me.

My auntie Chi stands across from me. She creases her eyes shaded under the wide brim of a straw hat, her face dwarfed behind the outline of a grey-plastic dust mask. She smiles with her eyes, noticing my lack of attention. Her look reminds me, keep awake, stay with us. She points to a gnarly-looking, furry black peach rolling on the sorting area next to me. Yes, that's right, throw it out, she indicates. I check on my mother who is below. She is balanced on her stomach on the edge of the bin with both feet in the air and her head near the bottom where the wooden slats patter with the thumps of peaches spilling from above. She temporarily defies gravity; she is a ballerina in the orchard, floating above the bin. Her hands move quickly. Peaches arch from her hands and out of the bin. This lot running by us is full of diseased fruit, and we three work quickly, tossing out what we know the cannery will reject. Our bins at the station will be graded, just like students with report cards, and our job as sorters is to keep the percentage of unacceptable fruit as low as possible without compromising too much loss in tonnage. We work, examining the peaches with keen eyes—a bird peck here, a spot of brown rot there, wind damage, skin scarring. Those are thrown. We process peaches from the last tree.

I hear the roar of engines at full power, the potential energy of an airplane on a runway before takeoff. I look at Rodney, who wears a hardhat and has cotton balls stuffed in his ears, see the strain in his eyes from calculations that must be running through his mind. He focuses on his father in the shaker, and I imagine the nonverbal communications being exchanged between them. Are the pads meeting? Check. No gaps? Close enough. Conveyor belt rolling? Right on. Sorting belt circling? Yup. A high pitched hum from the shaker engine precedes the hula-dance wiggle of the peach tree sandwiched in between two rubber clamps. Uncle Bob throttles the gas before engaging the force of the vibrating pads against the bark. Gada gada gada! He knocks the first fruits gently. They rain onto the pads, gathering speed on the cushioned slant before bouncing into the catching receptacle. A shadowy cloud of dust and insects vaporizes the air around the tree with the first shake, moving outward ever so quickly, precipitating with it an overwhelming feeling—the noise, the dust, the heat, the monotony. The cloud expands; it does not stop. I am smothered. After the first shakes Uncle Bob increases intensity, and branches and leaves jump even farther, flinging away peach fruits until the tree is bare. Manipulating the levers connected to the hydraulic arms, Rodney lifts the catching receptacle, then rotates the catch frame away from the tree, emptying the peaches onto a conveyor belt that trundles along the next batch of fruit.

The peaches ride atop the belt, stacked more than three or four high, moving towards me at the spot where they tumble onto a sizing screen that weeds out small fruit, spilling them through slots onto the ground. Looking behind, I see an orchard row littered with undersized fruit.

Peaches tumble in front of me, accompanied by the squeak and clank of chain scratching against circling rollers, some gummy from worm damage, others crusted from wind scarring. I am seeing life move before my eyes. I work madly, my hands constantly moving, rolling those little fruit balls, checking them for imperfections. Ouch! The rotating screen catches my hand and pinches a finger. I must fight to maintain ownership of what's mine.

It is easy to be distracted, mesmerized, especially in the heat, when the smoldering sun and rocking of the machine and noise lulls one into another world. After all, what is time and space? We count the peaches passing by us, count the bins picked, ninety filled a day, many thus far, so many more to go. We've moved down four quarter-mile rows the entire morning. Tree by tree, minute by subsequent minute. Sometimes time moves slowly and it is simply peaches, peaches, and more peaches I see along the horizon. I feel the weight of lunch settling in my stomach, watch the rippling waves of hot air shimmy above the catch frame engine's exhaust pipe. I hear the harvester machines singing lullabies.

gada gada gada gada

The shaker knocks and rumbles. Sing it quickly, as fast as you can. Sing it like choral practice, in 4/4 time, "Pearls pleased pretty Penelope. Pearls pleased pretty Penelope." Get into the rhythm. It comes from within you. Remember. Articulate. Shaker likes to rattle the edges. Shaker pounds a nice bass beat when it's knocking the tree trunks.

BRENDA NAKAMOTO

gada gada gada, gada
gada gada gada gada
gada gada gada gada
gada gada gada gada

The catch frame adds the continuous pitch of a high c with
the resonance and clarity of a bronze temple bell struck at
church. Meditative. Contemplative. A whine pervades the
orchard. One can hear the heartbeats of the harvesters a half-
mile away. From here the center of the universe begins....

Blond hair
blue-eyed David
charms the girls
in high school.

Athletic
brawn
brains
He has it all
Girls love him
I do, too

David
in my arms
against my skin
on my lips

...in my dreams.

Then there's George
who chases me

then dumps me
making out

after getting drunk
tossing up

not telling me
keeping it a secret

had it not been

for my snoopy best friend
who discovers everything.

Can I ever have a boyfriend?
How I want a boyfriend
How I want—

Brriitt! Just in front of me something crackles with the sound
of bending, ripping. The edge of the catch frame has snagged
a limb as Rodney moves forward. I turn, notice out of the corner of my eye a stout branch stuck on yellow painted sheet-
metal. All right, same routine done umpteen times before:
lift, help it slip away. Go forward, move it with both hands.
Brritt! Suddenly, wood buckles. I see rough, ragged bark filling my bubble vision, hear a snap, feel the sudden pressure
of the plastic frame of my dust mask against my face. Blink!
I don't remember screaming. *I can't help it.* It's all gut reaction.
My eyes tear, blurring. I don't feel much of anything, just
surprise.

Why is everything stopped and everyone looking at me?
My ears ring in silence; the machines are off.

Faces stare. The soft, plowed ground cushions my behind.
"Are you all right?" Rodney's eyes search mine. I'm all choked
up. I nod.

Fallen down on the job, no doubt, everyone must think.
My mother takes off my mask and wipes a tissue against my
bloodied nose. Stop bleeding. This is so embarrassing. I'm fine.
Don't mind me. My fault, I should have jumped off before the
limb broke, I wasn't paying attention.

"Maybe you should go home."

Go home? But there's work to do. I'm perfectly fine. It's nothing, really, only, I can't breathe very well right now. I hate a bloodied nose, the smell, the bad taste in my throat, the discomfort, and most of all the way it makes me look. Everyone, stop looking at me.

"It's all right, go home."

"I'm okay."

"You sure?"

"Yeah."

Mom smiles and nods. We're almost done. It's late in the afternoon. I hear the harvester motors start up. A tree shakes, fruits fly off the branches, and peaches tumble in front of me again. Now, where was I? Oh, yes, I wish I had a boyfriend, someone who I could call my own, someone who can see me for who I really am, but not how I am now, gawd, hide me from my friends.

The chatter never ceases.

I grab at a fruit scarred with blemishes and toss it over my shoulder. So many bruises before me, and I cannot keep up with all of them.

CARMEN

Carmen, where are you now; and Roberto, where have you gone? Drifting into the valley year after year, you followed the California harvests. Like a tide flooding the shore, pulled in and out by the force of the moon, you came and went, lapping the landscape with your whistles and laughter. Where are you, yellowed teeth, frayed hat, and bronzed skin?

A sun blazes overhead, filling the tired sky with white and a tinge of blue. Below in the shaded orchard, trees line across the field in manicured rows. It smells of fresh fruit, ripe and sweet. Men move from tree to tree, balancing lanky wooden ladders on their shoulders, side-stepping worn-leather work boots over dirt clods on the freshly plowed soil. Singing together, voices blend melodiously, weaving stanzas around the trees. Soloists occasionally digress into lilting arias. Others whistle while grasping quickly at peaches with their hands moving in continuous motion, reaching for fruits and plucking them from branches, then juggling them into canvas bags, removing empty hands again and matching their movements to that of their tunes. The men banter with each other as upward and downward off the rungs of the ladders they climb and regress, and all the while a sonorous drone of a tractor engine follows behind them.

How I've lost you, the Carmens, Robertos, Hectors, Humbertos, and Josés. The orchard back then sang with the vibrancy of your music. Your appearance mirrored the rites and passages of seasons, with summer my favorite, so full of voices and rhythm. In your nomadic life following the ripening of the crops, you probably thought no one noticed you, yet I did, Carmen. You twinkled your eyes and winked at me, sometimes sharing a stick of gum when you jumped onto the back of the pickup truck as we all headed into the field after lunch. I was the luckiest. Mom and Dad owned the farm. I was their littlest girl following in bigger footsteps, young and carefree. You had so much more at stake, a wife and family in Mexico waiting for you at home, dependent on your letters and what cash you mailed back. You had little choice, almost no choice but to cross that border multiple times—probably in the trunk of a car or by foot through chaparral and scant moonlight. By whatever resolve, you returned to earn some money. Such sacrifices you made. Now with a harvest complete, you are gone as a leaf withered and obscured on the ground. I cannot find you. How I miss you.

I have never told you before, and in secret I will tell you now. I admired the way you threw yourself into work amongst the heat, sweat, dirt and flies, with only a few stolen moments of rest—a quick nap taken during an afternoon break, leaned against the trunk of a peach tree with the rim of your sombrero pitched below your eyes. How you labored hour after relentless hour, in the dichotomy of the chill of predawn summer mornings and the sweltering of unforgiving afternoon heat. Helping us pick peaches, your heart shone. When Daddy got the scratchy-sounding phone call from you years later, Roberto, and in a very distant voice you said you had finally gotten a phony green card, a driver's license and a high-paying job working a lathe at a car factory in Detroit, I was happy for you. I knew you wouldn't have to move around anymore and could live in one place. And now, Carmen and Roberto, wherever you are, I want to tell you I think I had loved you.

ROBERTO

I heard a knock at the living room door and noticed two shadows on our front porch. I recognized one figure, that of Roberto, and I thought it odd that Mom then invited him in. What was the matter? Dad motioned for him to sit at our kitchen table, and in a moment, Jesse followed through the door. A big man, husky and broad with a protruding potbelly, he stank of cigar smoke and reeked of sweat and armpits. Jesse placed Mexican goodies on the kitchen counter for us as he walked in, a block of milk candy wrapped in paper, cocoa brown, smooth like caramel, yet hard and dry. I sliced a square of the confection, popped it in my mouth and sampled an interesting sweetness, a sensation though pleasurable also made me quiver. It felt like my teeth were chomping on aluminum foil. There was something inedible about this substance, a sort of electrical impulse I got from it. I sank my teeth into the morsel, could hear it squeak against the enamel as I bit. First reaction: yuck! Not exactly, but it was to say the least—different. I bit again, chewed and swallowed. For all its strangeness, I kept eating. And while I am anonymously in the kitchen breaking into the candy stash, I notice Roberto sitting next to Dad, and I can see his eyes sparkle when he talks. He is my Mexican Clark Gable, with a well-trimmed, cropped moustache, dark eyebrows, wide, brown eyes and smooth golden skin. After working in the fields all day, he has showered and slicked down his hair, transforming from scruffy farm laborer to a quite handsome man.

I glanced at Jesse and Roberto, and I thought how unusual it was for us to have guests. We were a rather private family; we didn't normally entertain, nor did we own the kinds of modern furnishings that most of my friends' homes had. I always thought it had something to do with our odd house, a refurbished military barracks from Beale Air Force Base sold to the public after the end of wwii. Dad had hammered and painted new walls for individual rooms, constructed a separate bathroom, living room, and dining room, and transformed the barracks into a home. There was always a tinge of imperfection shadowing our place, a kind of stand-alone quality that I wasn't exactly proud of. For instance, the table at which people were sitting was made by my dad, nailed with two-by-twos for legs and a plywood top painted in semi-gloss enamel and tacked with plastic laminate. Mom covered it with checkered-patterned oilcloth. Definitely, no one else had a dining table like ours. I was really rather embarrassed, though, Roberto and Jesse never hinted that our house was odd. Maybe we shared something in common, being poor; it's just that we weren't as poor as they were.

In that respect, I sensed an ease at which my parents interacted with Roberto and Jesse. There was always a comical tone between them. Roberto genuinely liked talking with Dad, and I could hear their mutual laughter, noticed how unusually comfortable my dad was with these men. In rare moments like this he became human to me. His attitude was a digression from the normal high-strung tension of his working days, especially during summers, when he was madly harvesting peaches. In that respect, the Mexicans became human to me, too, because they shed some of their mysterious layers wrapped around them and were within just a few feet of me, talking about everyday kinds of things like the dreadful summer heat, how they missed their families, how they planned to save enough money to buy a ranch when they could retire and return to Mexico. Jesse, for instance, liked dogs and wanted to farm. Most of what I heard I didn't pay much attention, thinking about how boring grownup conversation could be. But I learned things from being around them, listened to comments I probably shouldn't have, and I sensed that we from different cultures sometimes differed only by being born initially in dissimilar places and circumstances. How much we really had in common.

"Come, Harold, I show you something," Roberto had said and lead my father out the front door. From the porch window looking out onto the driveway, I saw Jesse and Roberto and

Mom and Dad at the back of the white Comet sedan we owned. It had been an auctioned state vehicle and my dad bought it cheap, for only $200. It became Carol my oldest sister's commuter car that she drove to Butte County Junior College a half hour away.

"See, this is how it's done. It's easy," Roberto must have said or intimated. I couldn't hear the entirety of the words being exchanged between my dad and Roberto, but I heard this loud thump, and when I glanced again, there was the trunk hood swinging wide open and Roberto right smack in the middle of everyone looking at him. There was an uproar of guffaws. My dad must have said, "Do it again!" because Roberto calmly closed the trunk, raised his hands shoulder high and slammed them down again, which somehow jarred loose the trunk hood from the hinge and made it pop open as easily if it had been done with a key.

Dad tried to do it, too. Roberto closed the trunk, Dad positioned himself at the back; he slammed down on the metal hood with both hands just as Roberto had done—and nothing happened. Everyone laughed.

After our guests left, Mom showed me what else she had learned. She wrote her name on a piece of blank typing paper, then tore a strip of wax paper and placed it over the writing. She rubbed the tip of a ball-point pen over the entire signature, pressing fine lines back and forth, scraping away the wax. She lifted up the wax paper, placed it down somewhere else on the sheet, and then rubbed again. In a few seconds, a duplicate signature of my mother's had transferred elsewhere on the paper. It was not a very good reproduction, and if you looked closely, you could see how she had missed some spots, but nonetheless I thought it a decent forgery.

I wondered how people had dreamed-up such things, how one could learn to cheat and steal. But I knew Roberto would never do that, no, not my Roberto.

My parents weren't naïve, though. I remember the great lengths they went to write workers' checks on a machine that stamped the amount payable in blue and red typeface and that punched tiny holes through the paper. Before imprinting the final checks, Mom, Dad and I had proofread each amount, calling out to each other the names of workers—Manuel, Humberto, Juan.... My favorite task was keying the numbers on the machine, pulling the crank and hearing the gears tumbling and then seeing the newly pressed and inked check.

Many years have since passed. Where is my Roberto, my Clark Gable? I imagine he must now be sixty or seventy years old. Maybe he is a grandfather, even a great-grandfather. Will he have remembered my dad, the Japanese farmer from Gridley? Can he recall that shy, impish little girl? Can he still break into car trunks and forge signatures?

ESMERALDA

How are you, Esmeralda, of cobalt hair, the shine and gleam of
igneous rock? Esmeralda whom I called Emphysema, because
that is how I think of you—not the meaning, just the sound—
and I regret my attempts to verify your name through school
records have come up short. I remember you. You live in a
silver bullet-shaped trailer, a mobile home gleaming grey,
the hand-rubbed burnish of aluminum foil. Your home sits
amidst the brush of the peach trees. We play together—how
I want a tiny bed like yours with a woven cotton blanket in
rich, broad lines of green, red, and white, with Mexican colors,
your favorite colors, like a flag. A window brightens the world
outside your pillow, opens to the outside; dogs and cats roam,
chickens peck on the bare, packed earth while a curious goat
forages and chews. A rooster crows. The sun shines and we
animate our dolls. I hold mine; you hold yours. Hands hold
one another. And we skip rope, twirl on swings—you in your
billowy, ruffled skirts and ankle-high white socks and black
patent shoes. I want to switch my home with yours that's not
much bigger than my bedroom. We dream beyond these trailer walls; I am a teacher or a nurse and you might be a singer
or a doctor. We drink punch and eat cookies together on top
of the bed, dotting the blanket with crumbs squishing into
our toes. How we laugh and giggle when the Mexican migrant
laborers smile at us and wave from across the yard.

A screen door swings wide. The wire spring screeches,
stretched taut, then whinnies and shimmies, slamming
shut. Flies circle lazily in the kitchen amidst the deepening
afternoon shadows. Beatrice, the farming contractor's wife
with plumped hands and meaty arms pats masa between
her palms. Stacks of corn and flour tortillas wrapped in wax
paper and foil rest atop the red- and white-checkered table-
cloth, next to a stove with refried beans simmering in a cast-
iron skillet. There is always food here; there is the smell of
sweet corn and the mixture of flour and lard and the flavor of
mashed beans and goat cheese. There is the texture of cream,

smooth and silky, and the warmth cast from the stove burner, blackened and coated in the charcoal layer of baked grease drippings. A tiny blue flame wicks underneath, ever constant, ever ready for the handiwork of the cook.

These tortillas melt in my mouth, the beans coat my lips, and I dream of no food better than this. Nothing can be better than this.

One day Mommy says I can't see you anymore, can't play with you at your house. I ask her why and she says simply, "No," but I believe it's because there are too many of your kind there, and for that reason she is afraid.

I see your class picture next to mine in the fourth grade, but absent in the third and the fifth. A flash of color in the peach trees you are, along with a giggling and a hand placed coyly on your cheeks.

My lovely Esmeralda, my Emphysema. Your fragrant breath blew in and has been exhaled from my lips.

I AM SANSEI

I am sansei, third generation Japanese American.

I am sansei, daughter of Hisashi and Masako,
who are called nisei, second generation.
I am sansei, granddaughter of Suyeno, Tamakichi, Hayawo,
and Shunjiro,
who are called issei, first generation

ichi—ni—san
one—two—three

The third follows the second, the second follows the first
Sansei daughter and granddaughter

I am

This Japanese language of the issei I hardly understand, for I
have been too far removed from a country I have never seen.
I know little of their ways or customs. Because of this, I sense
that I am a misfit centered in between two worlds—to America, the land where I was born and to the Asian world of which
I so closely resemble in my face, my eyes, my nose.

This sansei daughter carries a name with a specific definition.
San means three. I am three. I am of the third generation and
thus I am sansei.

At a gas station mini-market at the corner of Highway 99,
nestled at one of the intersection crossroads of Gridley, my old
childhood hometown, I wait in a car for my husband Shawn
to return with a soft drink and a chocolate bar. An old, beat-
up pickup truck passes by, crossing in an illegal right turn
through the parking lot to get onto the highway, whipping
across the asphalt, skating through the aisles of gasoline
pumps. The guy inside the vehicle glares at me. He yells,
"Ching-chong, Chinaman!" and this nondescript Caucasian

male with a baseball cap and plaid flannel shirt sitting in the driver's seat pulls his eyelids slanted using his forefingers. He mocks me. For only a moment I see him, because the truck passes by quickly, slowing slightly as it merges with traffic flowing north. Then he and the vehicle disappear into the mix of rushing cars. It is like I am watching something on television with me the uninvolved viewer—dumbfounded. I am touched, but I am not touched. The ruffian character I don't recognize, yet his wayward actions are unsettling. I reason, no need for me to get my feathers ruffled. After all, I tell myself that I am back in my old stomping grounds, a small town out of the hustle and bustle of the Bay Area and Sacramento, where I have lived for over thirty years. I used to encounter these kinds of things all the time as a child here. My reactions are rusty. That man was kidding—yes, that was all—but he reminds me of what I have so easily forgotten.

I guess he was supposed to be comedic. First of all, he's got it all wrong. The joke's on him. I am not Chinese. I am Japanese American. There's a difference, you know, the language, the native dress, customs, foods, and yes, our physical features. There are similarities, but there are strong differences. That man was a stupid idiot. That's that, and I mentally wash this distaste that settles in my mouth. But second thoughts, the ones that tear at you after they happen, speak otherwise. I am offended by something I cannot change. I know it wouldn't have mattered if I were Chinese or Korean or Mongolian or aardvark. He was making fun of me in a very personal way, in the way I looked, in my foundation of human biology of which I have no control.

When my husband returns, I relay what just occurred and he is furious. My tall, lanky dishwater blond lover wants to pursue the guy and punch him. It's a good thing that the other fellow was long gone, because an unbecoming scene was avoided. That's always how it is in times like this. I would like to disappear, to blend into the landscape and leave unnoticed. How I would like to think white, act white. I'm not this person

BRENDA NAKAMOTO

who people think I am, this seemingly demure female in a petite sized body. Oh how I can hate myself sometimes, how alien I feel inside this shell that I wish was not me. Good ol' Gridley. My hometown brings back so many memories.

Scraps of conversations, patches of images and words flutter into my consciousness, rustling in this wind of memory, the pulse and pull of that which cannot be contained. My mind swirls with misnomers, cases of mistaken identity. How many times in the past I've had to explain myself, to clarify my place of origin, because to others, the beginning of my ancestry confuses them. I am not normal. That I've been singled out so many times makes me callous to questions about my origin or race. I have not been ridiculed in a long, long time. Ching-chong Chinaman inspires commotion.

Someone had asked me:

"Where are you from? The Philippines?"

"From Gridley."

"Reedley, down south?"

"No, it's Gridley, just north of Sacramento,"

"I mean—you don't look like you're from here. Are you from Korea?"

"No," I carefully reiterate my answer. "I was born here. My grandparents were from Japan."

"You speak really good English."

My patience is waning. I try to answer politely without this sharp edge rising in my voice. I say, "I was raised here in California. My grandparents were from Japan."

"You speak Japanese?"

Will this person ever give up?

I try again, rewording my answer, "No, I can't speak that language. I'm from Gridley, a small farming town between Sacramento and Chico."

"Oh?" he says in a voice that is quickly losing interest.

My questioner looks at me with raised eyebrows, he is puzzled. How disappointing I must be to him. I get this feeling that I am just not proper. I am all backwards. I should be more Japanese. Why go around looking like something I am not? I am a hermit crab creeping under someone else's shell. The charlatan within me at times plays up to her image. My uniqueness grabs attention, just like what's written in my high school yearbook that's collecting dust on my bookshelf. Amidst my classmates' signatures, on a corner of a page is boldly written—

"To the cutest little Jap girl in our class. Luv—"

It is a compliment, even considering I was the only Jap girl in our class. I know the issei and the nisei certainly didn't appreciate being called Jap. Yet I take no offense. In my eyes cutest rises above the others as if in capital letters sprinkled across the page. Someone thinks I am cute. Me, this short, stocky little girl with sharp bangs and big round head and husky figure. Why, I'm like one of those dolls stuck on top of car dashboards that the Mexican low riders drive with their boom boxes roaring, my oversized head bobbling at every stop. People like squeezing me, pinching my round cheeks and exclaiming how huggable I am.

"Hey, fatty," says Jerry with sky-blue eyes and wavy, blond locks, poking his finger into my side. He's standing behind me at the playground drinking fountain. I have been sweating, jumping rope with my girlfriends and swinging at tetherballs.

BRENDA NAKAMOTO

Drops of perspiration roll off my forehead and down the front of my stylish cat-eye eyeglasses. I continue washing down water, taking long and steady gulps.

"Uh-huh," I mumble.

"Hurry up!" he says, "What are you? An elephant filling up a trunk!"

I stop swallowing. That's a new one. I am used to being called some far-out names, and I try to believe that sticks and stones can break my bones but names will never hurt me, that I've grown a thick skin. Nevertheless, ouch. Sometimes one or two sting all the same. Actually, all of them sting, it's just that some sting more than others. I step aside, give up my spot in line and let that lousy Jerry grab the shiny chrome handle to the fountain spigot. Before I go, though, I turn around and glance at those blue eyes, those delicate waves of hair parted to the side that drape across his brow. He smells of sweaty boy just like I must smell of sweaty girl. Do I despise him? Of course. I can even hate him this very moment. Yet as much as he irks me, I've got this soft side and...and couldn't he be cute?

You betcha.

And snot-faced boys with dirt-stained t-shirts and big clown feet hold a coveted place in my heart, despite what sometimes comes out of their mouths. But Jerry will never notice me, not his little fatty. I avert downward my eyes when we pass each other so that they will not meet his.

If who I am is reflected in what I do, then this sansei daughter is an urchin wandering the streets, seeking little notice. How I want so much to blend in, to mix with the dull grays and browns of this earthen landscape. Don't make me different; don't call me anything, not sansei, not fatty, and not elephant with a trunk when all I ask is to live unnoticed and be like everyone else.

MELODY AT SUNRISE

An unsteady groan and buzz cuts through an early-morning quiet, the calling and whine of a crop duster at work. The chop of propeller blades reaches out, then disappears, as a plane flits from one side of the field to the other.

I lie in bed and listen. How I long to be up there with it, somersaulting in the vast sky.

Again, the duster buzzes overhead, saws back and forth over our peach orchard, until its vibrations fade into the distance. Through my bedroom window, I see puffs of marshmallow clouds resting against turquoise. After the plane leaves, a lonely hush settles in. A dove coos.

I wait. I anticipate, hoping for a refrain in the next passage of music.

AUTUMN

FALLING LEAVES

The lazy days of summer drag to an end, puffing stiff gusts hot and sultry, with drab skies stretching across the horizon. These shifting winds charge through the valley floor in whistling bursts, fueled by an uneasy change in temperature. Autumn knocks. It is a time of farewells—harvest is over— and farmers move on to other things: to plowing fields and repairing and storing equipment before the air chills and winter storms move in. Sometimes fall slips in subtly, with a nip in the morning air and dew on the grass, the cooing of valley quail, the barking of pheasants and the distant cackle of geese strung overhead in v-formations. This weather is a reckoning, a balancing of things changing and ending as well as a subtle welcoming of the new. Although, with any change, there is not always a clear-cut transition distinguishing one from the other. That's how I'd always felt about the end of harvest. Working through those hot summer months took utmost diligence and conviction. Then passing to the end of the season left me feeling stranded, as if clinging still to that other world.

Mom was in the kitchen doing her Mommy kinds of things, wiping down the laminate countertop with a washcloth, drying the plates and cups from our last meal. She paused, draping the dishtowel over her shoulder and sighed, a sharp lilt of irritation in her voice.

"Tell Jesse the pickers are leaving too many peaches on the trees. We want them cleaned off the branches. They're putting everything in the bins, marbles and all, giving me heck when I sort, tossing out the seconds. They know better and are going about their sloppy ways as usual. It's going to cost us money! You need to do something about it, honey," Mom said. She tells Dad what to do.

I hear a grunt, that and the slam of the back door and the thud
of my dad's leather boots stomping down the porch steps.
Mom turned to me, wringing her hands on the dishtowel.

"You know he never listens to me, not to a word I say! All hard
headed and thinks only of himself!" She fanned herself with
her hand, her face flushed in the height of menopausal fury. I
didn't say anything, just stood there and listened to the window air conditioner whining in the living room and drowning out all outside noise. It was hot and dark inside this little
house: curtains drawn, windows shut tight. Only the living
room stayed ice cold, while the rest of everything else sim-
mered in heat.

"Mom, that's just how he is. He gets this way every year," I said,
in my futile attempt to calm her. We were in the tail end of
peach picking.

"Well, I don't like it. I don't treat him like he treats me. Why, I
used to laugh a lot the years before I met him. Now look at
me, all I do is complain." She grimaced and opened the cabinet door next to the sink, twisted open the white cap on an
orange-tinted plastic bottle and popped a bi-colored hormone
pill in her mouth. The edges of her lips turned down when
she gulped a glass of water. "You know, the only reason we
stay together is because of you kids."

What could I say? Hard to beat that. And I, probably being just
as pepped up with hormones in my adolescent years as what
was in those little pills, quipped, "Then why suffer? Who cares?"

She shot me a wild look, one that pierced through me. I wondered whatever happened to my Mommy whom I used to hug
and rub my head against a perfumed cashmere sweater that
she wore in cold winters, so soft and warm and sweet.

No one could blame either Dad or Mom. Irritability was something one learned to live with. At harvest, anything could go

wrong, which ultimately meant lots of yelling coming from Mom or Dad. We think we've had enough: like, okay, I'm tired of handling and picking peaches all day, all week, all month, seems like endless months. Can't we just leave? I want to catch a movie, jump in the canal, inner tube down the river. There's no time. Dad is strung out. Mom tries hard to adjust.

The tractor was leaking oil; the forks on the forklift bent to the side and turned down. The hauling truck wasn't starting up in the morning without following a list of crazy antics: pull out the knob of the choke, push three times on the gas pedal. Turn over the ignition, let it whine a few times with the button pressed hard under your thumb. Pump the pedal again. The engine complains: whoa, whoa, whoa, mmmm. Keep it going. Listen for the catch of the pistons and crankshaft sparking on their own. Hear them firing, faintly. Pedal down to the floor; there's a grumble, it's happening. Now let up on the gas. Hold out the choke. Keep it there with the engine on the verge of sputtering and drowning, then slowly push in the choke while throttling the gas. Not too much, not too little. There it goes, the truck engine idles on its own. Don't dare gag or cough or the gas will flood the compartments and we'll have to start this whole process all over again.

Everything had something wrong with it and everything couldn't get fixed, not now, not in the height of harvest. No wonder Daddy threw wrenches.

Dad stormed out of the house and to the shed just as Jesse Hernandez and his dented pickup truck rolled into our driveway. Jesse's arrival was usually for reasons not good, either that or else he wanted something. His pickup squeaked and shifted around the corner, brushing against the limbs of the trimmed cypress hedge that marked our entrance off the county road. Two big dogs in the back bed pranced from the tailgate to the cab, testing the air with drooling tongues. Jesse with an oversize woven straw sombrero toppled lopsided on his head, squeezed a pear-shaped torso from behind the steering wheel. A hairy beer drinker's belly poked from underneath the hem of a dingy white t-shirt. A shadow of un-shorn beard dirtied his chin, and pockmarks, nascent scars of childhood chicken pox, cratered his cheeks like the face of the moon. His forehead glistened in oil.

Jesse shook Dad's outstretched hand and glanced at the inside of our shop, which was covered with its usual layer of dust. In summer nothing stayed clean. And hidden in that quick glance, I could sense this burning desire, this sort of envy that Jesse the labor contractor had towards my father. Noth-ing of Dad's was particularly that valuable or interesting to me, they weren't things I would want to have: an arc welder, grinder, vice, acetylene torch, air compressor, wood stove, ladders, metal milk crates, truck doors, and even spare bum-pers. But Jesse's eyes lit up when they fell upon the weathered motorcycle parked in shadow in the corner of the shed.

"Harold, you never ride that old BMW anymore. See, it's rust-ing. But you know what, I give you good money for it. I give you a deal, take if off your hands. Fifty dollars, no more. Wouldn't get that price from anyone else. What do you say, Harold? You should sell it to me."

Dad joked, "You can ride a motorcycle? Nah. I'm sure you wouldn't want to break something."

"I can steer with one hand. It's easy."

"No, I don't want to sell it." Dad hid an irritated look on his face, his cheeks reddening.

"Come on. Look at those old, cracked tires. Hey, fifty-five dollars—I give it to you right now." Jesse pulled out his wallet, thumbing his fingers through a wad of bills.

My dad would hold his ground, but I could see the wheels spinning in his head. He really didn't ride that motorcycle much. Aside from using it on the orchard roads when he was out running the irrigation water, it was just sitting there in the shop. But fifty-five dollars was way too low a price. Besides, he didn't want to just give it away, not to Jesse, anyway. But that particular conversation faded when Jesse introduced a new topic. That was the way Jesse did business, breaking in the important news amidst the everyday chitchat.

Jesse said, "I lost four men yesterday: Diego, Ramiro, Miguel, and Joaquin. Immigration raided camp. Everyone ran into the orchard, but those four didn't make it out in time. They were caught with no green cards, and now they're gone, getting shipped back to Mexico." Jesse looked at Dad, straightened his back.

"So you'll have other men for me tomorrow, won't you?" My dad pulled the oil and sweat-stained ValleyChem baseball cap off his head and put it back.

"I'll see. Marvin Stowe needs a crew, too. And the workers who are left are complaining they're not getting paid enough. They want more than four dollars a bin." Jesse struck a match on the sandpaper of the matchbox and lit the end of a fat cigar. He put his lips around the tip, inhaled slowly then blew out. "You know, Harold. I always like doing business with you." My dad shifted his weight. You could smell the peaches, feel their overwhelming presence—hundreds of them on the branches next to our house. They were waiting. And now we had eight fewer hands, four fewer able bodies to get the peaches from our orchard. But what could he do? My dad did what he always had to do, tried to smile, throwing in a joke or two to appease Jesse, to make gentle conversation, because at this point, our farming life hinged on our contractor's ability to get more workers.

Dad paid the men the higher price they had asked for; he waited for the Mexican replacements that Jesse miraculously drummed out of thin air. And the peaches were picked, bin

BRENDA NAKAMOTO

by bin, truckload by truckload, and eventually the ferocious summer air cooled and fall drifted into the valley.

My dad's high-strung temper faded with each passing day after the end of harvest. I didn't hear him barking orders to everyone, so common the last few months, cursing foul words at Uncle Bob, my mom, even the dogs and cats. Tools didn't fly across the shop floor, and he didn't need to peel out of the driveway, leaving lines of rubber from the old Ford pickup truck bleached to the color of a faded dusty sky.

Autumn rolled in, the leaves started falling off the trees, and my parents could again speak to each other in civil tones. I could actually see my father's face now, not buried under a coating of dirt and grime. After school one day, I stepped inside the front living room and found Mom and Dad sitting on the couch, hand in hand, holding onto each other. Mom smiled, Dad grinned. The room was dark, the window curtains drawn. I didn't know what to make of this. Such affection. It was so foreign. Parents were so unpredictable.

I slipped into the kitchen, grabbed a bag of M&Ms and started munching. If I wasn't careful with the chocolate I could break out in zits. But hooray, summer was over, fall was here, and I had a good feeling inside. The flurry of autumn winds mixed in with occasional zephyrs frizzled my hair with static electricity. But I didn't care, not one bit. The winds marked success, a completion. Harvest was over. We had made it through another year, and that was reason enough for celebration.

Harold and Brenda Nakamoto

BOUNDARIES

During the rainless midsummer, peach tree branches coated
with a thick layer of dust sag downwards, their limbs droopy
and weary as if having endured too many days on an arid farm.
Under a whitened, hazy sky and next to the rumble of tractor
and vehicle engines that thunder nearby, those trees closest to
the dirt road suffer from these windborne particulates, from
mites and other insects that hitch rides on flying dust particles amidst the grating force of gusty winds. That is life on
the edge. These trees are the front line. They are unprotected.

This boundary of the orchard is where parallel, vehicle-traced
tracks outline a fluffy path of finely ground earth separating
one property from the next. This road is where I walk, where
I obtain solace on my way to watching sunrises and sunsets.
I launch and end my days on these roads. I see far into the distance, peer at the skyline over the Coast Range and the Sierras.
Here I sense proportion, a comparison of where I am in rela-
tion to other landmarks. The edge of the orchard, the boundary, is where space opens up and I inhale. I look outward.
Following this road takes me elsewhere. This orchard road I
call mine. It is not county road or city street or someone else's
private property. I bend down and pick up a pinch of dust,
lay it on my palm. Blow. Away it goes; and what once settled
on my hand is now traveling somewhere unknown: down
to the next tree, off flying to the water pump, perhaps going
towards a neighbor's field to settle again on a leaf for another
day. Dust turns my bathwater brown. It recycles from earth
to shoe to air to tree to air to skin to eye to mouth to hair. It
changes what it touches. My tongue licks my lips where dirt
has mixed with salt from my skin. Tastes gritty. Grains of
dust grind between my teeth.

In the early morning, from moisture left in a scant morning
dew, a thin crust forms atop the powdery road, like that of
baked bread, the molecules of soil and water strung together
in a fragile cohesion. I walk this orchard road, breaking a

trust, shattering topsoil with a trail of footprints that I leave behind me. Each step penetrates through crust and powder, crumbles what little support the water had given back to this earth, and my traipsing scores the road and kicks up a little firestorm of dust. Step, step, poof, poof. My solo journey creates reaction. I fill the air with tiny particulates. I am making my imprint on this land. Dust flies, it swirls. Underneath my feet, soil lies flattened, blurred, compressed down from what mixture it had been before. There it is. I can see the name brand of my tennis shoes written on the soil. Keds, Keds, Keds, Keds, only it's stamped in backwards. What a delight. I am leaving behind a trail of words zigzagging down the road in my bow-legged stride. The dust settles back down, but always to someplace different, to be blown away in the next windstorm, perhaps stuck into a crack of a tree limb or wedged between the tread of a tractor tire. In the height of summer, this powder kicks up around me, letting loose, swirling, bending, and curling in currents. This cloud at my feet moves as if alive. Each of my actions arouses a reaction, an active dust cloud, booting away all that will not cling to the earth from gravity. Only one thing won't change, and that is that nothing stays the same.

I walk the road around our peach farm. How tired these trees look! Skeleton limbs arch before me, with leaves ratty and already starting to thin and drop to the ground. Late in the harvest season and stripped of their fruit, the peach trees stand hobbled. There is nothing more, no other purpose left, but to prepare for winter dormancy. I miss them. They will withdraw and leave. I will not be able to talk to my trees. They won't be there to listen. The spirits in this orchard will no longer notice me. Tears well on my cheeks. The arrival of autumn and winter pains me now more than the actual change. Silly me, I think, wiping my fingers under my eyes. Only silly girls cry like this, and for what? For trees. The newly observed chill in the morning air along with dew on the grass is an omen portending a time of slowing down. Rest. That's right. We need rest. And mommies and daddies can start to think about snuggling close under thick blankets with the days shortening and the nights lengthening. When summer ends, there will be less activity and fun, no more time spent driving tractors or watching the big trucks hauling fruits to the grading station. No more fights throwing peaches and prunes. For now, my feet kick up powdery soil. They sink deep. More than just my footprints cover the road. In the dust are the punctuated signs of a frog hopping, a snake slithering an s wriggle from one side to the other, an egret splotching w-shaped footprints next to the lowercase w's of a California quail winding its way north, and the light, dotted line of a beetle skittering. Everywhere I look, I see traces of life. This road is no longer just my road. It is all of ours. It is a highway. These footprints permeate the road left to right, up and down, as if chaotic characters on paper. Secretive animals—pheasants, snakes, rabbits, coyotes, and raccoons—venture out mostly in the night and early morning, when we humans are less likely to see them. I cross over the indentations around me—v-shapes, m-shapes, flower-indented paw prints, squiggles marked with stops and turns—and I imagine that which had gone on their merry way before me. I stop and bend down. I find fresh heron footprints—why, they're as big as my hands!

I travel farther on the road, on the side that borders the almond orchard owned by the colonel. The colonel who retired recently from the air force bought this property, fulfilling one of his dreams of becoming a farmer. Behind his back, Daddy snickers and jokes with Mommy about how the colonel should have stayed a colonel because he doesn't know anything about how to raise almonds, not having farmed or worked in agriculture his entire life. Some of the almond trees are sickly, oozing a gummy sap from their trunks, mysteriously losing leaves and then dying. That orchard is in trouble. However, there is one thing for sure: the colonel can certainly raise ground squirrels. The excavated mounds of soil from their burrow systems are popping up everywhere: in the neatly stacked piles of chopped wood, at the base of the valley oak, in the roots of the almond trees, and underneath

Daddy's water pump. Daddy curses, "Damn squirrels!" when he sees them cross the border from the almond orchard property onto ours. Sneaky squirrels with fur color matching the soil blur back and forth as shadows crossing the road, leaving in their wake almond shells littering the ground, chewed in half, hollowed, with just enough space for me to squeeze the tip of my little finger into.

Squirrels and humans compete for these nuts that are now ready for harvest. Maturing in late summer after the last of our cling peaches have been picked, almonds will soon be shaken from their branches, swept into rows and vacuumed up by harvesting machines. I pick an almond from a branch. The dried outer husk separates easily between my fingers. Then I open wide my mouth, place the shell between my back molars and squeeze down, chomping with a penetrating crack through the shell. Parts of it crumble onto my tongue and I chew and spit, then pry open the shell with my fingers. An oval nutmeat falls into my hand.

Long before I can even get close, a squirrel has already sounded an alarm. *Chireep!* he says and flattens himself low to the ground, dragging a scruffy tail behind him and scampering ahead to the safety of a burrow. Others cross from the irrigation pump and return back to the trunks of the outer row of almond trees, where they have constructed an underground latticework of tunnels, little hillocks of excavated soil piled against the base of tree trunks. "Run, run, run!" the squirrels bark. The boldest ones, the sentries, refuse to go into their burrows and position themselves near their entrances, sitting upright with their paws tucked close to their chest when they chirrup, *Cheery-chicka, chicka; cheery-chicka, chicka; cheery-chicka, chicka.* They repeat in an abrasive long sentence. They bark. It's a definite scolding; it sounds like wheezing, like that of a toy rubber duckie squeezed between my hands. I have trespassed into their realm, for they conceive of no borders or boundaries, cannot understand the full meaning of a powdery road dividing our orchards. Our side is to the west.

BRENDA NAKAMOTO

Yours is to the east. Stay on your side! That is fair. But by the time I wander past the chirping squirrels and they are many yards behind me, my glance backwards shows them already crisscrossing our road again, stamping footprints in the empty spaces, stirring up more dust, reclaiming what is theirs.

I pass the north end of the orchard where our trees butt against Marvin Stowe's peach orchard. If I were to continue walking farther north, in a little while I'd wind up at the next paved county road, the one that leads to my old elementary school, and I'd have taken a shortcut of sorts through the area, because the farm fields are like little checkerboard squares between the county-maintained asphalt roads. I am told that Mr. Stowe one time brought my *baachan* [grandmother] back to our house in his pickup truck after finding her lost in the rows of peach trees on his property. Borders blend, boundaries erase. Can't I, too, get lost? If yes, I wonder if I may find my way back again. So I stick to my dusty well-traveled path. This is my line of safety that will always lead me home.

The west end of our peach orchard is my favorite part to walk. It is next to an irrigation drain ditch and borders a wheat field. It is where I scare up mallard ducks. A pair bursts out of the cattails from the gully alongside me, the air whistling through their wing feathers, the male with a shiny green head, the female, a drab brown; and they angle into the sky like tilted bowling pins. As always, I stop and look to the southwest.

When I see the Sutter Buttes, I can't help but feel they are an integral part of my home. They are mountains I've seen always outside our kitchen window, the base of the foothills only fifteen miles away. The eroded remnants of a volcano created 1.5 million years ago, with the highest peak 2,000 feet above the valley floor, the Buttes changes with the seasons. In winter and spring they are grassy green, occasionally frosted in snow. In summer and fall they mature to a golden hue. It is this color I see now. It is the staple color of harvest: the golden glow of sprays of mature wheat, rice and oats, the background pigment of ripe peaches, and it is the last flush of the setting harvest sun sparking off the ridges of the Coast Range. How golden is farming! It is my way of life. It is my world. I breathe it daily, from the break of dawn over the Sierra Nevada to the setting of dusk on the Buttes.

The memory of recent peach fuzz clings furry and thick. When picking peaches off the branches, the fuzz flies off the fruit, into the air, clings to sweat, gathers in folds of skin, in places not ever thought to have wrinkles. And the itch! I cannot escape. So my mind tries to block out feelings, to forget the heat and the sweat. After a full day's work, the dried rivers of perspiration outline salt etched on my neck and forehead and the back of my shirt. I walk this dusty road, taking deep breaths filled with smells of recent memories. Even with the peaches harvested, the air is still scented.

I am back home, finished with my walk, poking about my dad's shed. I like the feeling of this place equipment and farming implements stored on shelves, lining the walls and scattered on the floors. I kick up dust coating the cement.

"Here, Skipper, here kitty, kitty! Where are you?"

She darts out from an old oil drum stuck in the corner of the tool shed. She's hidden her kittens safely behind them. In that back room where the dust swirls and floats in eddies through the lengthening rays of afternoon light, I hear her babies mewing.

"Come on Skipper, I've brought you a bowl of milk."

Poor bedraggled Skipper purrs and rubs her body on my shins, temporarily leaving the confines of her birthing quarters. I reach down and pet her long, gray hair. A mix of Persian and stray, she is a cat with large black eyes, a moist, pink nose, and shaggy hair around her face that stands out like a mane. Long hair and a farm cat don't mix, and unless brushed frequently, her coat soon knots with burrs and stickers, and her entire undercoat is matted into lumps against her skin. The only way I can remove them is to cut them, which is difficult, especially when I accidentally slice her with the scissors. Then, she won't let me touch her anymore. She runs around looking like a chopped-up cat, dark gray strands mixed in with ragged jags of silvery short hair. I cannot keep up with the sticky seedpods and foxtails that tangle within her fur. This cat should have been an indoor cat, not outdoor, especially here in weed country. But I let her run wild, and my lines of ownership holding her to me fade. Her kittens are just out of reach, and they even hiss and snarl at me with closed eyes and tiny open mouths. I press my face against the empty oil drum and stretch my hand into the darkened gap between curved metal and the wall. I cannot reach far enough. Without the human touch they have already taken another step away from me, back towards a native, undomesticated state.

Skipper hides her litter amidst the riffraff of farming implements kept in the shed. In that tool room, hoes, shovels, axes, pick axes, augers, and rubber mallets stand on end against the wall. It smells of grease and dirt. High above, rolled burlap sacks and aluminum picking buckets hang from hooks under the rafters. How safe and at home my cat feels living amidst this clutter.

I lift docile Skipper into my arms, wrap my hands about her small chest hidden in all that frizzed fur and lay her on my thighs as I sit cross-legged on the cement floor. Her nipples are erect and still wet, her breasts swollen with milk, the hair around them matted flat from recent suckling. I pet her forehead, tell her how much I love her, how beautiful a cat she is. The sound of her purrs increases and she turns her head to the side, inviting me to scratch behind her ear. She warms my lap and kneads her claws into my pants. They prickle but don't hurt. Skipper's eyes close and I see the faintest outline of a smile creased on her lips.

Suyeno Nakamoto (Baachan)
working in tomato fields

DIRTY DIRT

A fire that burned down a house branded marks on the skin of my baachan. She had scarred arms, wrinkled and jaded from years of farm work, hoeing, weeding, and spading under a harsh sun. In splotches on her legs and forearms, white skin blotched against tanned brown where damaged tissue, void of pigment, had healed over burns.

I was told she saved a life that evening of the fire. Almost everyone in the family was safe and outside, except my Uncle Ray, still in a crib. *Ojiisan* [grandfather] boosted up Baachan to a tiny open bedroom window that she squeezed through, and she re-entered a house licked in flames. Barefoot and in nightclothes, she came out with Ray in her arms. Then she ran over a half mile down the road to the nearest neighbors, begging for help. The next day a doctor with tweezers pulled bits of gravel from the soles of Baachan's burned feet.

I burned myself this morning with a drop of boiling water on my hand while making coffee. It stung later when I stepped into the bath for a warm shower.

I knew her only in her later years, in older age, when she cat-napped waiting for meals at the dining table and on the couch and in her darkened bedroom smelling of cedar and incense. She played pick-up sticks with me, scattering the toothpick game pieces with short, stubby fingers too accustomed to hard labor and unfamiliar with delicate tasks. That's why I could beat her. She was too strong. I laughed when I won, that I, a little girl, could outsmart my grandma. She laughed, too; I sensed that her loss and my accomplishment pleased her.

We hardly talked or exchanged words. Somehow that kind of communication wasn't necessary. What words spoken between my mom, my dad, and her were in Japanese. Though my baachan lived in the same house, I could never strike up a conversation, not even ask a simple question like, "How are you today?" It was as if we were living on different planets. I didn't wonder much then. I could think only of playing games and picking up the next plastic stick that she and I were competing for. Come on, Baachan, it's your move. Now that I look back at it all—remembering, hearing the shuffle, shuffle, shuffle of her slippers scraping the linoleum floor, the creak and groan of the wood foundation giving under her weight—in a way, I sense her presence now more than I did then. As invisible as she seemed in real life, decades later she is painted vividly into memory.

She stands alone with the peach trees, body curved over a hoe, hacking at weeds at the gnarled trunks. She's there when I leave on the school bus in the morning. She's there when I return in the afternoon.

"She shouldn't be working. No reason for it," my mother complained to my father.

"Let her do it. It makes her happy."

Mom searched for Baachan in the orchard when she didn't come home for dinner. Baachan lost track of time. Later, we three daughters and Mom and Dad and Baachan would sit around the kitchen table in silence. That was the Nakamoto kind of family dinner, not much verbiage. I'd hear her slurping food, especially the soups or stews with gooey soy sauce and sugar and salted broth. When she brought bowl and chopsticks to her lips and scooped savory delicacies, I listened to that which was *oishii* [delicious].

Baachan never stopped working. Even years later when she moved to a nearby rest home, Baachan in a cotton dress pulled diligently at the lawn grass. She bent from her waist and stooped over the ground near her toes, fingertips plucking at the leafy blades of green.

BRENDA NAKAMOTO

"Tell your mother to not pull weeds," the management had scolded my dad. "The men are looking."

That rest home, a little house off a county road, couldn't have held more than a dozen residents. Dad told this story to me with a quiver in his voice, tears in his eyes, at having to admonish his mother for doing something that gave her joy, gave her a purpose in life.

I cannot let go. I am a part of her. She resides in me. Sometimes when the north wind blows across the valley floor, scattering clouds and clearing out the horizon of everything except frosted blue sky, I think I hear the voices of my ojiisans and baachans drifting above the open spaces at the edge of town. Nah, it's only you who you hear in your head, my husband the scientist insists, just you.

Dad boasts about how poor he was as a child. Ojiisan purchased rice in fifty-pound sacks, twelve at a time. When money was short, he stretched the precious rice by mixing it with barley. Mice chewed into the bags and Baachan sorted out the *nezumi no pon pon* [mouse poop] from the grain. She cooked on a wood stove, over a packed dirt floor, and Dad remembers her sometimes dropping food, bending over and scooping it up with her hands and serving it. Nothing was wasted.

At a dinner party, my sister Arlene repeats something Mom said: "There's dirty dirt and then there's clean dirt. Dirty dirt is city dirt when you don't know if someone spit on it. Clean dirt is farm dirt out in the orchard."

It easily could have been me whom my baachan saved when she slid through the window of the burning house. I conjure up my grandmother and think I see her, hear her, feel her. I read a draft of this story to my father, who listened with eyes closed. I asked what he thought, and he opened his eyes and replied, "My mother was a great person, wasn't she?"

*Masa Nakamoto (far left, first row)
at Jerome, Arkansas, internment camp, 1944*

BRENDA NAKAMOTO

SHIKATA GA NAI

My mind wanders when the lazy days of summer are dragging to an end—hot and sultry, white, drab skies stretching from horizon to horizon. I contemplate the whys and the howcomes of life. In a vacuum of knowledge, I am left to imagination. Many things are uncertain. I want to know what made my grandparents come to California back in the early 1900s. What was it that drew them to this valley of hills and swales bordered by mountains on each side? It might be appealing, yet not particularly in summer, in the heat of a hundred degrees in these simmering, languid dog days before the turn of autumn. My ancestors moved here for some reason. They left Japan, sailed across the vast Pacific Ocean and somehow braided their lives together, scraping a living from this land in the Central Valley. That I know.

My parents and my aunts and uncles couldn't tell me much about my family history, and I thought that unusual, so cruel for a child who wanted to learn about what she was and how she had come to be. "We didn't talk much with our parents," they said. "It was long ago. Too busy working, too busy getting food on the table. Children were to be seen and not heard. Papa came after us with a switch and beat us when we were bad. He said 'No' when we asked for candy." When I tried to pry stories from my uncle Bob, he curiously told me he couldn't remember. My mother said the same thing. It was only my father who later solved the mystery by telling me my uncle was offended, that my uncle Bob thought my questioning about his past was none of my business. That was one of my early experiences delving into my genealogy. I learned to keep quiet and squelch my inquisitiveness. That in itself was not the best of solutions, but it did make me start reading on my own about California history—poking about the great halls of the university library and breaking open tomes written about the Japanese immigration to California. I began the arduous task of reading dry text filled with statistics and graphs and all sorts of numbers, some of which was eye-opening, but mostly eye closing if I stared too long. However, I did begin to get an idea of what might have been an integral part of my cultural past.

"*Shikata ga nai* [It can't be helped]," is what Baachan had said to her son, my uncle Bob, during wwii on that bus ride to a Japanese internment camp in Amache, Colorado. She was not the only one who used this phrase; many of the other issei were heard saying it. Those few syllables told me so much about her and the lives of those who were getting evacuated: that she must have accepted some good with the bad, that although she was in an unfortunate position she could do little about, there was a part of her that might have been at peace with the conflict. Baachan and her family were going to live in tarpaper barracks behind barbed wire, not knowing that would be their home for several years. Nothing could be done. Baachan was native Japanese. Her American-born children—with the exception of my father, who was drafted into the U.S. Army—were ordered to evacuate. Shikata ga nai. Sometimes circumstances like this cannot be helped.

I see a gibbous moon and stars emerge behind her in a night sky, and houses and cars and trees blur in the rushing wind passing outside the train window. Others in the rows around her have drawn their shades, blocking out their views, shutting out the outside, so that passersby can't see in, won't see these foreign-looking people with slanted eyes getting carted away like cattle. But Baachan keeps her window open. And I see the moon behind a grandmother who is rocking in motion to the rhythmic movements of the rumbling train, with hands folded, salt and pepper hair pulled back into a dainty bun, adorned in a favorite cotton dress she likes to wear that shows her ankles. She closes her eyes, maybe even smiles, and hums a Japanese tune, drowning out the monotonous rumble that is transporting her away. And I am being taken away, too. Shikata ga nai. Maybe I can understand if I try. Thank you, my dear uncle Bob, for relaying what you could, for I know I have trespassed onto personal territory.

BRENDA NAKAMOTO

Most of what I knew about my grandparents I had to imagine, I have to surmise—like putting a dry sponge into a puddle of water. I soaked up what lay around me. It may not have been pure, it may not have been clear. I knew that my baachans married as picture brides, exchanging their photos with my bachelor ojiisans living here in America. Dad thought my ojiisans must have paid a lot of money to get my baachans to leave Japan. Obtaining a wife was not trivial. This arrangement was facilitated by families hiring a *baishakunin*, a matchmaker, who acted as a mediator between the future husband and wife. It was done solely with the exchange of pictures and letters.

For me as a female, third-generation Japanese American, I cannot help but wonder what kind of social pressures could have caused my baachans to agree. I wonder if it could have been love at first sight. Not likely. Perhaps the women were promised fruitful lives living in a fertile valley surrounded by mountains and forests and prairies and rivers, where one might live an easy life. Also just as unlikely. Perhaps my baachan, had she stayed in Japan and not moved away, would have scraped an impoverished life of squalor cramped in a tiny hovel. It must have been cold for one living alone in Japan, the chill of winter permeating through thin walls of a small house. Maybe my baachans feared life as spinsters. Perhaps parents needed money and simply sold their daughters. Alas, some things such as this I may never fully understand.

My baachans might have wanted to leave their Japanese families behind; they might have wanted to start a new life in California, with its promise of adventure and independence. Only this kind of fiery attitude could have sustained them for the hardships they would experience ahead, for surely, I do know how much social and physical pressure my grandparents endured here: as cooks, as gardeners, as farm laborers, and at whatever menial, odd jobs they could find. My father's mother's scarred calico-patterned skin on her legs and arms bore the reminder of her daring rescue of my uncle from a burning house. I keep a picture of that same baachan in a memento box as she appears decades later, irrigating row crops and standing by a ditch flowing with water, dressed in a man's baggy clothing with a shovel in her hand.

My musings may be for naught. There is little written about my grandparents, only what scant genealogical information my mother-in-law Virginia gleaned from her resources: death records, census data, and immigration records. I think, wryly, that it took a white person to find the birthdates and birthplaces of my grandparents. No one in my family knew exactly. During the time of my grandparents' emigrations, the late 1800s and early 1900s, Japan was undergoing radical changes in their social system. Life was hard, money and food were scarce. People did what they could to survive, and that, I surmise, might be ultimately why my baachans and ojiisans left Japan to come to California. It was a hunger.

I imagine the tremendous amount of fortitude it took to step on the boat that carried them from Japanese to American soil, forever, for my grandparents never returned to Japan. As far as I can tell, they broke off ties with their families, not that it was purposeful or because of ill feelings, but I could find not one of my living relatives who knew of any of their kin in Japan. They just weren't talked about, and as time passed, connections to the homeland were lost. Records of my lineage stop at Hiroshima.

Would it have mattered if I had known my grandparents were seasick from the long voyage across the ocean or that they were bunked below ship huddled together like sacks of potatoes? For me, it would matter a great deal if I knew how they had felt, because now I can only imagine. If I listen long and hard, I can hear women weeping, voicing complaints, and I can smell *nigiri*, rice balls wrapped in seaweed, offered as solace to those who were missing their homeland, frightened of what they had done to themselves by agreeing to emigrate.

BRENDA NAKAMOTO

Maybe it is me who is not so determined, me who has softened because I have been given a life rich with opportunities—and it is partly because of the hard work of my ancestors. I believe they carried a certain kind of spirit, a candle lit through darkened avenues. They could not have known what pitfalls lay ahead, what kinds of suffering lay in wait for them. When I think of my grandparents, I think of endurance. It is something I don't have, not like they had.

My dad was named Hisashi by his parents, because in Japanese it means long life. Before he was born my grandparents had lost two infant sons and a five-year-old to disease or illness. Hisashi was their first male child who survived past childhood.

At age fifty-seven, Ojiisan, my mother's father, killed himself with a handgun, just two months before my parents' marriage. Dad told me he believed Ojiisan killed himself because the money from the strawberry harvest had been gambled away; he felt himself a failure, unable to adequately provide for his family. He was ashamed. My dad had said they lived like Okies.

Ojiisan, if you can hear me now, I do not think you were a failure. Without your fortitude and perseverance, I would not be here, and for that I am forever grateful.

Ojiisan, my dad's father, died in a hospital in Gridley during wwii, isolated from people of his kind, because all persons of Japanese descent had been relocated to internment camps away from the West Coast. Suffering from tuberculosis and unable to leave the hospital, he stayed behind, confined to a bed while the rest of his family except my father was interned. My dad's last communication from Ojiisan was a letter sent to him while he was stationed at an U.S. Army base in Australia. The letter said, "I am scared. I am so alone."

No, Ojiisan, you are not alone, not now with me hearing you. Your voice entwining with mine carries across a windswept breach in time. You speak through me.

There is a certain kind of greatness I connect with my grandparents. I see them as noble and worthy people, even though my knowledge of them is limited. I imagine that a part of my heritage is from something much more than just myself, perhaps because it all feels so inanely purposeless to think of life as anything less. I am here now because of what others before have accomplished.

This kind of thinking happens to me after the dog days of summer, the lazy, stretched-out period of time following the harvests, when most the production of food has left the fields. The work of the farmer for that season is almost complete. The lives of my grandparents are done.

I think back to previous autumns when, as a child, I walked the perimeter of the peach orchard, the sole basis of my parents' livelihoods, and I talked to the trees with their leaves turning amber and falling to the ground. I told them that I would wait to see them again in spring. I carried this heavy sense of longing for something lost that I wasn't quite sure of. Now I know why.

It isn't logical, yet in a way, that's how I have always felt—that things continue to change, that life moves forward whether I like it or not. Some things I wish I could hold onto longer. And sometimes I think I see the glimmer of what might lead towards eternity.

Seattle, WA. *Passenger and Crew Lists of Vessels Arriving at Seattle, Washington, 1890-1957.* Micropublication M1383: line 14. RG085. 357 rolls. National Archives, Washington, DC.

BRENDA NAKAMOTO

SEARCHING FOR GRANDFATHER

Here is an email from my mother-in-law, who is researching my family's genealogy. She sent me the information below that she had discovered about my family. The following is regarding my grandfather, my mother's father.

Hi Brenda,

I've found Shunjiro Sakaoka in the passenger records of the ship, "Minnesota." Below is what I found in the index, and attached are the two pages which list him on line 14. His mother's name is given as "M. Sakaoka" [who lived in] Hiroshima.

These records are not easy to read. It is easy to get one line mixed up with another. On page two, there is a description of your grandfather: 5 feet, 2 inches tall with brown complexion, hair and eyes. He lived at Nihojima Mura, Hiroshima Ken, Japan. His father paid his fare, and, while the boat was bound for Seattle, the ship would travel on to "Frisco," where he would disembark. From there he would go with the $50 he had to Sacramento. He was 17 years old, and apparently had to leave his mother in Japan in order to join his father in the U.S.

— Virginia

Shunjiro Sakaoka, my grandfather, my ojiisan, I never knew you. A self-inflicted bullet separated you from me before I was even conceived, before Mommy and Daddy were even married. And I would never be able to rock in your arms or drool on your shirt or make gurgling sounds in your ears or see your lips crease into a smile or hear your hearty laugh.

Instead, many decades later my mother-in-law finds traces of you in the ship's registry of the Minnesota, which departed from Japan and docked in Seattle before arriving in San Francisco. There's only sketchy information, but now it's like I can start to see you—a young man with a few bills and coins jingling in your pocket.

Is it too late to tell you that I think I would have admired you? I would have loved to hear you tell me your stories, to have felt your burly, husky arms around me in a bear hug. My ojiisan, I could have said. Even now, the words sound foreign on my lips, because I never had one when I was born, only bits and pieces of ideas of what a grandfather would have been to me.

Would you have said that you dreamed of touching the stars and that's why you left Japan on a ship bound for the infinite east? That you watched your mama running along the wooden planks of the dock in her zoris with your baby brother bound on her back and she is waving goodbye and crying, "I will remember you, Shunjiro. Good luck and farewell, my son."

Would you have said you planned to return to Japan after making your riches, enough to dress your mother in the finest kimonos and cover her pantry with multiple sacks of rice? And you and your father would have wrestled the gold off the California sun and pursed it in your belongings to send home? Instead, Shunjiro, were you prepared for what lay ahead? Long days as a farm laborer or as a piecemeal worker, many homes come and gone, war, internment, loss, drinking, gambling, and not even electricity or indoor plumbing.

I imagine you smiled big on that ship, feeling the brisk salt air on your face, the sun on your shoulders. So young and daring, you were, my ojiisan. You were not tall, but when I think of you, I think of a big so huge, I cannot put my arms around it, I cannot grasp the all of you, the boldness of you, with the heartrending kind of feelings that might have accompanied leaving your mother—forever—I must imagine. And you made a go of life here in California, like the rest of the emigrants soon to populate the state. Dreams dreamed, some reached, some squelched in disappointment, some forgotten, hardened into the bitter alkaline crust of a beaten dirt road.

Shunjiro, why is it that I want to know you? It must be that you left too soon, in a fit of disappointment, in a reactionary state of being. Oh, I cannot disguise my own disappointment.

But there you are in the ship's registry; there you cannot hide from a curious historian's eyes. Though it gives me but sparse information, I feel that I am wrapping my arms around you, my ojiisan, my hero, my adventurer, my inspiration. Oh beloved departed, I wish you could hear me.

Shawn Smallwood with gopher

BRENDA NAKAMOTO

VARMINT

A warm-blooded and furry creature no bigger than a human
foot, the pocket gopher feasts on roots and herbaceous matter,
spending a life of seclusion amidst tunnels underground.
Expect no muttered *oohs* or *aahs* from those who occasionally
see him, for he has been given a special name: we call him
vermin; we call him varmint.

Equipped with fur-lined cheek pouches that conveniently
close fully behind ever-growing incisors, and thus considered
one of the world's most naturally productive earthmovers,
a single pocket gopher excavates to the earth's surface more
than a cubic meter of soil each year. For this he is despised.
He burrows into the soil, constructing intricate mazes of ver-
tical and lateral chambers for living and food storage, pushing above ground all that has been removed underneath.
This act is the source of his disgrace.

"Look!" my mother wailed.

I followed her finger pointing out the kitchen window to
where a patch of dicondra grass sported little umbrella heads
underneath the walnut tree. She motioned to three mounds
of bright, moist soil splotching her lawn. They had popped up
overnight in the same way pimples did on my teenage face.

"Gopher!" she bemoaned. "My poor lawn. Look at what it's done."

I didn't think it was all that bad, just a few piles of freshly
overturned dirt marring the deep green of cultivated lawn.
Our German shepherd quizzically nuzzled her nose in the
soil; then, a few sniffs later, waving her rump in the air followed by some vigorous tail wags, she cleaved apart one gopher mound, flinging earth and grasses in all directions. Later, I shoveled the topsoil off the remaining mounds, trying to
squash back into the burrow all that the gopher had brought
up. That made the blotches even larger. Yet, if that wasn't

cosmetic misery enough for my mother, in the next few days, new mounds appeared. Persistent and patient, the gopher had repaired tunnel damage and performed home maintenance, innocently sparking a battle between human and beast.

The garden water drizzling from the end of a hose and plunging deep into the gopher tunnel disappeared somewhere, but nowhere visible, into a dark and unknown recess in the earth. For over half an hour, water blasted into the hole, never to be seen again. I listened to liquid gurgling and to the kicking on and off of the water pump that kept filling a tank hidden under a whitewashed wooden gazebo. I expected something to happen; there was nothing, only this realization that, indeed, it must be true. If one dug deep enough and long enough, they could reach through the world all the way to China.

With a life spent mainly in the soil, a gopher senses things in a different way than we who live above ground. A gopher cannot hear well or see well. Instead, he communicates with the world using long facial whiskers in search of food or finding mates. The hair-like bristles touch the earth, picking up vibrations and movement; they orient him within his burrow system. How I sometimes wish I could navigate confidently in the pitch dark, finding my own way as he does.

We rarely see them, but we observe the most obvious signs of their existence: burrowing. The ground blossoms with irregularity where the gopher has been at work, punctuating its surroundings with holes and hillocks. With incisors that beg to gnaw, a gopher manipulates the landscape, predictably unpredictable in transporting earth from here to there and there to here in a manner most unbecoming to human eyes.

Blame him for irrigation diversion, sending precious agricultural water from one side of the field to the other or worse, out into the street. Blame him for your twisted ankle when you trip in one of his holes. Blame him for levee breeches and flooding. There aren't enough human fingers to plug them.

BRENDA NAKAMOTO

See, a gopher truly earns his infamous reputation.

Some things mean business, though. Punch a hole with a nail. Push in a fuse and strike a match on sandpaper, lighting the wick to a smoke canister the size and shape of the inside of a cardboard toilet paper roll. Stuff this and the fizzling fuse into the entrance of a gopher burrow. Throw on top a few shovelfuls of soil, stomp it down, and compact it into a dense wedge. Wait to hear the initial boom of the chemicals igniting and watch the wisps of smoke discharging between the granules of soil. Then walk away.

I did just that. I, just an innocent farm girl, was working with hazardous chemicals and smoking these poor gophers dead.

Well, now, I guess I wasn't so innocent.

Though, if you ask us now, my dad and me, we'd both agree, it's a tough life, the farming life. Later in his retired years, Dad sometimes referred to himself as "a poor dumb farmer." I suppose one most regrets that which they didn't do, the risks not taken, the achievements not fully recognized or fulfilled. If Dad had had any extra time while not tending to our farm, he might have done things differently, relaxed a little, indulged in fun. Maybe he would have gone to college. He had always wanted to be a pharmacist, not particularly the farmer he became, enslaved in a lifelong career raising peaches just so that kids like me could grow up happy. Out of his sense of honor, Dad might have felt he was destined for that farming occupation the day his father ordered him as a teenager just graduated out of high school to work in the migrant farm labor camps, forgoing a college education. Ojiisan needed help supporting the rest of the family. I was told that every week thereafter from Dad's graduation, Ojiisan visited the migrant camps where my dad was working, collecting a share of the pay; and Dad followed his father's bidding by staying in the farm fields of the northern California valley, treading on a path that extinguished any hopes for a different kind of life.

Maybe dreams can change. One's regrets morph, just like peach blossoms falling and peach fruits fattening. I suppose if Dad had never touched a peach tree or nurtured the fruit from bud to maturity, I might not be here. In some ways, it feels like something has shifted down to me. Dad has passed along this heavy weight; I find myself rattling on and on about the farm, the trees, the summer sun as if there is no end.

Some things need to be born, some burdens carried, then let go and exhumed, which brings me back again to the subject of those darn gophers and other pests. There are definitely no guarantees about anything. That's why the farm pests, those varmints, garnered no respect.

Tiny tracks crossed from trees to water pump and back. Densely packed footprints crossed, spraying out in disorganized profusion. Footprints stepped on top of one other, underneath wind blown sand and dust; and the patina of old tracks flattened into obscurity, painted by the elements.

Over the years, the squirrels in the orchard multiplied into permanent fixtures in the almond trees. Sentries barked alarm calls, sending residents of the colony scattering underneath woodpiles and structures. They were annoying; they were smart; and they were destined to be another of the targets of my innocent vengeance. Those darn squirrels stole our nuts. One chattering squirrel scurried beneath the almond tree. I kept my eyes on him, knowing I had to be quick.

I smoked squirrels just as I did the gophers. Dad paid me, and I thought little of doing my dirty work and packing chemicals into the almond orchard we had recently purchased from the colonel. Same sequence, same routine. Pull out a fuse, pop it into a small hole punched by a nail and secure it into the canister, light the fuse, plunge it inside a burrow, then move on. I pushed one sizzling wick and canister into the ground under the trunk of an almond tree, where the entrance of a squirrel burrow joined together with the exposed fingers of tree roots. With my hand, I tapped it in as deeply as I could and then buried it under loose soil, using a shovel.

Whump! You could hear the muffled explosion of the chemicals igniting. Then a faint red glow along with smoke wisped out from the base of the tree. The bomb burned hot and I watched and smelled gas seeping through the cracked spaces of crumbly soil. In the heavy, windless summer air, a murky cloud of poison thickened around me, shrouding me in a fog.

Then it hit me, maybe for the first time, how ridiculous this all might be. I wondered what I was doing. Engulfed in poison, was I now the beast? It was as if my considerations had turned sideways. I could not retrieve the smoke canister, could not stop the burning, could not scrape my shovel under the guts of the trunk whose main roots lay just above the smoldering smoke bomb. I heard the crackle of wood catching fire.

The burn lasted awhile. I waited, a prisoner of sorts wrapped in my own thoughts. I remember the sky darkening and the evening advancing, and I eventually picked up my goods and left with a pained feeling. I never told Dad. I returned the next morning. The fire was out. I pushed away the loose soil and looked inside the hole and discovered corrugated clumps of charcoaled wood clustering the innards of the still warm tree trunk. The almond tree stood erect and tall and the upper canopy had not burned; the leaves in the branches were still peppered with nuts. Everything else seemed the same, but I knew it was only a matter of time until the rest of the tree would succumb to the damage. Have you ever wished you could somehow turn time backwards?

"Would you mind helping me with my research?"

My husband Shawn asked me to assist him with a project. He was going to China for a conference and couldn't do some time-sensitive work in an alfalfa field. I was in the last trimester of pregnancy with our first child and I was staying at home. The work he assigned me was easy: place a one-foot-square iron frame over designated spots in the alfalfa field, snip the vegetative growth, put the plant material in a bag, tie and mark. Simple. It was called sampling, collecting information from various spots in the field. The research, of all things, was about gophers and their effects on alfalfa production.

I bent down on the ground with an extra-large t-shirt of Shawn's stretched tight over my stomach, rubbing against my exposed belly button. I squeezed the handles of the grass clippers and scissored them back and forth within the alfalfa plants, cutting the vegetation just as he had instructed me. Our son kicked as I knelt. It wasn't just me now in the alfalfa field. Our little boy was working, too. My belly literally sat on my lap. He was growing quickly, starting a new life, and in a way, it was fitting that I was in this field back in agriculture. I had missed this kind of life since leaving home after high school graduation, and I thought I would never look back, especially since my parents had sold the farm. But this day felt like a good day. I was at ease again, under an autumn sun burning off the morning dew. A pair of Swainson's hawks soared overhead, catching thermals in the late morning as they circled and leaned into the wind. I thought about Shawn halfway around the world doing his science, and here I was, working on his behalf, snipping alfalfa.

"Everything revolves around gophers," he would tell me later. He admires them; he thinks they're cute. He's studied how to eradicate them in forest clearcuts, he's familiar with the kinds of poison baits used to kill them, he knows of their cycles of fecundity and the normal cyclic progressions of their populations through the seasons.

"You can't really control them," he says. "Kill all of them in a

BRENDA NAKAMOTO

forest clearcut or an alfalfa field, and all you get is an invading population of immature sub-adults who disperse from the perimeter, taking up residence in vacant burrows in even denser numbers." Not only that, he admits he's discovered how beneficial they can be. Their tunnels take irrigation water deep into the ground, directly to the roots of the legumes. Those snippets of alfalfa plants sampled from near the gopher systems in the alfalfa fields after analysis proved more lush and vegetated than those not growing on gopher burrow systems. That darn varmint was a better irrigator than we farmers! Farm girl was never destined to leave that farm.

In a short paragraph in a magazine article, scientists reported their discovery of the first signs of life after the volcanic eruption of Mount St. Helens. After the explosion that blew off the top of the mountain and incinerated an entire lake into water vapor, after a mudslide of hot water and debris swiped off the ridge top, after an entire forest was sliced apart like kindling sticks from sheer magmatic force that covered the area in deep ash—the first sign of life in the aftermath was that of the pocket gopher.

That pocket gopher, that diligent construction worker, protected deep underground even shortly after the decimation from the explosion, continued to steam shovel with chiseled teeth and sharpened claws, bringing up soil from far below the ash—soil rich with seeds, the living memory of the forest—and he deposited them onto the scarred mountain surface. And with that sprang forth the wildflowers, the insects, the bees, and the songbirds. Then came the hawks and the creatures up the higher predatory food chain, and blown-up Mount St. Helens would eventually see life again on its crippled face, because of the mere pocket gopher.

So who now is varmint? A pocket gopher who insistently inscribed a mark upon my landscape is steeped in muses rich and clear. He is life inscribed within life itself. For me, gopher, continue to dig deep and awaken; teach me again how to see.

Harold and Masa Nakamoto dancing

BLURRING

Daisy, a mutt mix of rottweiler and Labrador retriever, romps through the junk pile next to the farmhouse in what looks like a lot filled with going-extinct farming equipment. She yelps and sniffs, nuzzling her nose into splintery piles of old two-by-fours.

Apparently left abandoned and starving out in the orchards, she arrived at Dad's doorstep a bag of skin and bones, shortly after the sudden death of my mother. Dad fed and cared for her as his own, soothing his fingers on her furrowed forehead, just as he might have fondled Mom's hand when he walked her onto the dance floor. Granddaughter Breyon, my sister Carol's daughter, visited Grandpa and subsequently named the dog Daisy, saying she was the spirit of my mother sent from heaven to ease my dad's heartbreak. An angel from nowhere, Daisy brought joy to Dad's newly solitary life.

Sweet doggie, play; enjoy the warm, autumn day with pale blue sky and quiet air, sunning fence lizards and the smell of drying walnut leaves. I sweep piles of crispy, fallen leaves from the lawn, just as Mom had done for us each lazy autumn.

"No, Daisy, no! Drop it!" A bundle of brown fur attached to a white clump of a cotton ball is clamped in Daisy's mouth. Daisy runs purposefully towards me, brushing against my legs, taunting me with her recent catch.

It's a bunny, a cute little cottontail. "Come here!" I chase. Daisy prances side to side; she thinks this is a game. I grab her tail, clutch her by the scruff of the neck, press my fingers at the hinge of her jaw, force her mouth to release its victim.

The bunny drops to the ground, only to slither a few inches in disjointed fashion. It is now two bunnies as the front legs shuffle relentlessly and the hind legs drag lifeless.

Shawn cradles the bunny in his hands. "Poor bunny, sweet little cottontail. Bad dog! Mean dog!"

He looks at me with a sadness I cannot describe. The bunny looks at him with bulging eyes of desperation. Shawn asks for a hammer and walks to the back of the shed, to where a bunny burrow is tunneled under the cement foundation of the outhouse my dad had built for the migrant workers who used to work on the farm. Shawn comes back later empty handed.

Bunnies used to live with me; Mom used to live with me. We were once all together. How I had loved them and how I now miss them: Mommy, bunny, dog, and angel. At times like this, a sudden blurring makes me unable to discern any difference.

A THREAD INTO TIME

Time plays tricks on me, threading the now to the then,
stitching together fabric of mental bits and pieces. I live in
a double world, formed from my compulsion to hold onto
a past, to my defining childhood moments that are fading
from memory. I cannot keep them close forever; I think if I
lose them, I lose parts of myself. I sometimes wish I were still
back on that farm, living on Dad's land I had considered mine,
when I could touch and own it. Sometimes I think I have
never left.

I call my dad on the telephone and hear a voice that shakes.
It wavers in pitch like a string of a violin with the bow drawn
slowly, the musician's finger on the strand trembling ever so
slightly. Time passes, the sun rises and sets, the moon waxes
and wanes; I'm not a kid anymore, and I have only one parent,
Dad, and he is still living at home in the little farmhouse.
The orchards are sold and all that is left is a white stucco house,
the shed, and three acres of land. My last tie to agriculture
is there with Dad, where I can visit him on what's left of our
parceled-out property. Only then do I feel like I've got farming blood. He lives on a county road a mile long amongst his
handful of neighbors. Thank goodness Uncle Bob stays in a
small house at the end of the street. The two brothers remain
close. All of us kids grew up and left. We did what we were
supposed to do: pursued better-paying jobs than what our
peach trees could provide.

I listen to Dad's faltering voice on the phone line. It's an older
voice, a more distinguished voice, one that has absorbed years
of abuse with yelling directions and orders. I hear no sense of
urgency in it anymore. It has no punch to it, not like when he
was farming, when everything was harried. We were always
late. Dad had run his business and our lives, pushing us like
lemmings jumping off a cliff. Years later, with the land sold
and Dad now in a home that's paid for in full, with nothing
but free time on his hands, one might think he could finally

rest and be happy. His punishment was over, all debts resolved. But there was one thing missing: Mom died.

"You know what gift Mom gave me that I am forever grateful?" Dad asks me on the telephone one day, during a talk we are having when I am trying to check up on him.

"What's that?"

"She made me learn how to dance. If I hadn't learned how to ballroom dance, I wouldn't have anything to live for anymore, I wouldn't have the friends that I do. My life revolves around dancing now." His voice fades and a silence follows. It is a silence filled with unspoken thoughts. Although our voices are quiet, I know our minds are churning. My mom must still have this uncanny ability to connect with us. She was always a busybody, one who kept my strong-willed dad in line. She was the one who insisted my dad start dancing, to get him to exercise his prosthetic knee after the surgery.

"The doctor's orders," she would say about Dad. "He needs to work that knee and learn to keep his balance."

Mom was Dad's crutch after the knee replacement. They walked together down the street, elbows locked, leaning against one another like lovebirds. I knew better, though. Mom was helping Dad maintain his balance, keeping him from stumbling and falling. She had her motives. Shortly after his surgery, she enrolled in ballroom dance classes, and a new routine emerged into their lives among the doctor visits and physical therapy sessions: dancing. They had never done it before in their lives. Within months, I watched my parents transform magically into accomplished dancers. Soon they were driving up and down the valley floor catching engagements at the senior centers and at the Moose and Elks clubs. They liked live brass bands and gathered together with other people from miles away to listen to them play, while they danced atop polished wood floors of the dance halls. Saxophones, trombones, clarinets, and horns. From Paradise to Chico to Yuba City and Sacramento, dancers flowed across those voluminous enclaves with the scraping, light, rasps of tapping shoes swooshing against wood, keeping beat to a snappy tune. Men and women entwined about each other twirled as singular units. *One*, two, three, *one*, two, three. Waltzers flowered in circles.

For Mom and Dad, a brand-new world opened in their retirement. They met people just like themselves who had worked hard their entire lives. Now, in their golden years, they started to relax and enjoy.

Mom and Dad danced with heart and soul: my dad the once-gritty farmer, my mom the simple farmer's wife. I couldn't believe it. Mom is in a flowing polyester dress and Dad is in a gray suit. My eyes follow their movements on the dance floor. It is like they knew each other intimately, their fingertips touching, Dad pushing gently with his palm and twirling Mom in his arms. Her skirt flares up, exposing some underskirt and leg. She unwinds and spins again. At the end, she takes a couple steps back, rotates her hips to the side, matching her footwork with his, hands and fingers touching. Then they are back together in the swing again, left then right, pushing and pulling.

I break the silence on the phone and say, "Sometimes it feels like just yesterday when I was watching you two dancing."

My dad's voice jumps. He answers, "And we got pretty good, yessiree. I don't want to brag at all, but we were better than most. Some old folks know only a step or two. Mom and I could do lots more—slow or fast—we could improvise. It's a matter of listening and feeling the rhythm. That's what we had that other people didn't: rhythm."

Yes, Dad, you and Mom had definite rhythm. It was not just with dancing, though. There is that thread pulling me back again. I wonder why Dad doesn't mention anything about farming and peaches, about how they hung together through all those dusty, dry years, rainy years, frosty years, more years than their dancing years multiplied thrice, decades, listening to the howl of the north wind and the pummeling of rain and hail on the rooftop and spending umpteen Christmases at my aunties' and New Year's at our house. How their nerves frayed apart through the harvest seasons, then somehow mended back together in the off seasons. Yes, Daddy, you and Mommy had rhythm.

"I agree," I say. "You two were good with each other, really good. If she were here right now, things would be so different. If only we had known about the hardening of her arteries before the heart attack, she might be alive." My mind is talking aloud its thoughts. I am speaking without really thinking. How my life is littered with regrets, scars ever present in the raw. The moment I utter my last words, I hear the tone change in the sound of Dad's breathing. He clears his throat.

"I don't want to live no more," he states flatly. "I want to go where Mom is."

"You don't mean that."

"There's nothing left for me. Nothing for me to look forward to."

"You have dancing."

"There's not always someone to dance with."

"Maybe you need to find something else to do."

"Like what? I don't know what to do."

I can't argue or persuade. I know better. My father will not budge. Bullheaded, that's how he is. If there is one hurdle that my dad hasn't jumped in retirement, it is knowing now what to do with his life. I can't believe it—my father not knowing what to do. I remember that we kids ran when he roared his orders. But that was back then, years ago. He never let up. He sacrificed all of himself then so that runt kids like me could be here now. Trying to think of hobbies for him late in his life is almost a joke. Truth is, my dad needed that work not just for the money, but for other reasons, for himself. That's my belief. Farming was his life. Mom was his love. The two go hand in hand. I know it. I feel it. I won't say it. Now, though, if I were Mom, I'd be talking sense into him.

I sigh. Dad doesn't notice, can't hear the tone of my disillusionment. I don't know what to do, either. I won't admit it. I am grasping at memories as much as he is, trying to touch that which was once tangible. Like the wind blowing, the dust and leaves swirling, my thoughts gyrate and I can't tell Dad how to be happy, how not to miss Mom, how not to be lonely. Never before have I been in the position of trying to make a decision for my father, to be on the other side telling him what to do. The roles are reversing.

We go forward in a medium of constant movement, forging through in our process of making choices and stepping from one landscape into another. Sometimes for me it is as if time bends. I look back and see the peach blossoms and the first push of green leaf buds from yesterday at just a hand's grasp away. I can almost touch them, yet cannot.

My dad is no longer talking with me, probably leaning his elbows on the table with the telephone propped next to his ear. Instead, my mind watches him walking briskly through the plowed dirt with a shovel balanced on his shoulder, crossing up and over levees that wind in jigsaw puzzle patterns across the orchard. It is summer and Daddy is irrigating the peach trees. I am little and I toddle clumsily behind his giant footsteps. He shows me how high the water has risen, to just inches below the top of one check. The peach trees within are saturated in water. It is hot and humid in this forest of trees.

I long to take off my shoes, pull up my pants and wade my bare feet in that warm and squishy water. Daddy thrusts the shovel into the levee, using the weight of his boot and strength in his arms to sculpt away soil. The water cuts a thin line at the top, and he pushes it through by raking his shovel across the mud. A small waterfall cascades down as irrigation water escapes from the boundaries of one check into another. It quickly cuts a wide break and ripples in rapids towards me. It rushes at my feet, creeping in wiggly squiggles like a snake. This chocolate-colored froth frightens me.

"Daddy!" I yell, and I scamper up the ridge of narrow dry soil on tiptoe, watching the rushing floodwaters brush around the rubber soles of his hip waders.

He laughs, wipes his brow and returns the shovel back onto his shoulder and steps towards me. I clamber onto him piggy back, giggling, wrapping my legs about his waist, my arms about his neck. I am safe with my daddy, safe amongst the shade of the orchard under the boughs of the peach trees, safe in this moment where time seems to never touch me.

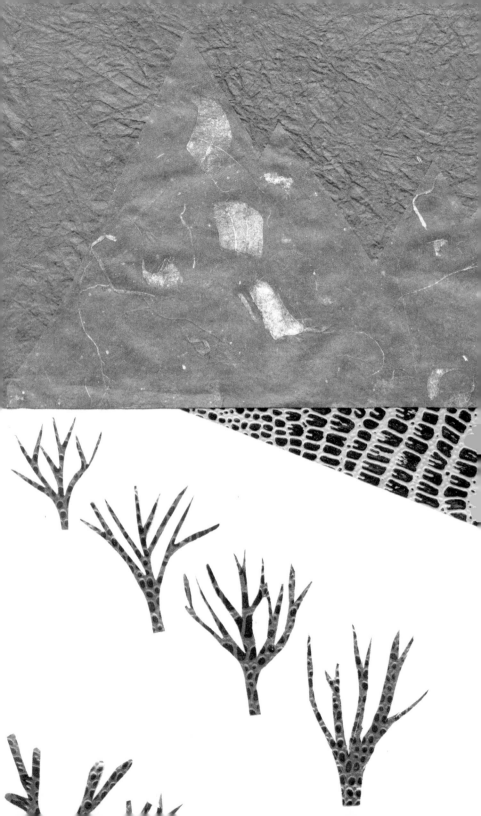

WINTER

OKAZU

The Japanese have a dish, similar to goulash, called *okazu*, which literally means side dish served with rice. I've not seen a recipe anywhere like the one prepared in our family. It's one Mom used to cook; she called it our poor man's sukiyaki. Not made with thinly sliced steak or shiitake mushrooms or yam noodles or bamboo root, our okazu was from cheap ingredients always on hand: hamburger, potatoes, yellow onions, and whatever else one found available. Brown the hamburger in a skillet with oil. Chop onions and sauté until translucent. Cut potatoes into one-half-inch chunks. Cover the fried hamburger and onions with a shallow layer of water, add potatoes, and bring to a boil. Place a lid on top and simmer until potatoes are soft. At this point, additional sliced vegetables can be added, such as green beans, asparagus, green onions or eggplant from the garden. Add soy sauce, sugar, and salt to taste. Boil a few minutes more. Spoon okazu with lots of broth over a bowl of hot, steamed rice.

Mom and Dad loved okazu. I wouldn't admit the same for myself. I ate it because it was what Mom served. I really wanted to be more American, which I was, of course, third-generation Japanese American, but I wanted something more defined, something readily tangible, like having blonde hair and blue eyes and being tall and thin like my Caucasian friends, not the short, stout, and dark figure that stared back at me in the mirror. I wanted American food: hamburgers, hot dogs, fried chicken, and French fries that I was convinced my friends' moms served every day. Instead, I got okazu.

There's nothing quite like waking up in the morning to the smell of soy sauce, vinegar, and sugar. That with the obscuring pea-soup tule fog of the Central Valley in winter is quite a combination. The day before New Year's, Mom started cooking at 5 AM and wouldn't finish until early evening. She called this making the *bentoo* [box lunch] for the next day. We Japanese celebrated the New Year holiday with an all-day feast of delicacies: chicken teriyaki, *sushi, sashimi, tempura, mochi, koko* [vinegared rice, sliced raw fish, deep-fried vegetables, rice cakes, and pickled white radish] and an assortment of appetizers such as boiled shrimp and octopus. In the middle of frosty winter weather, pungent odors wafted underneath my bedroom door and settled around me, odors inescapable and trapped inside. They were strong enough to wake me and drive me out of my warm bed. With the smell of soy sauce and vinegar, I didn't need an alarm clock. They were not gentle, not like the aroma of pancakes or toasted bread. In the early morning I wobbled into the kitchen where my mother was humming and hovering over pots of steaming liquids and chopping vegetables on a thick wooden cutting board. Live clams soaked in a pot of salted water. The purple head of an octopus flopped sideways over a tangled mess of legs. Fish scales peppered the porcelain sink and a deep burgundy side of raw tuna sat on a plate ready to be sliced. The kitchen windows fogged and sweated with condensation on the inside, and outside was just as obscured, enveloped in fog. All I could see in the thick mist were the outlines of naked peach tree limbs and an occasional lone hawk perched on top.

I grew up. Along with my body, my taste buds adjusted to Asian foods, and I eventually accepted my fate being connected to a Japanese culture, which I couldn't escape from, anyway. I don't think I appreciated all of my mother's efforts to indoctrinate me until I realized I was about to graduate from high school and leave home forever. Slowly it dawned on me how closely linked I was to the farm, the fog, the trees, the dry valley heat, and even those pungent sweet and sour smells from the kitchen. I knew barely a thing about cooking Japanese food; I had depended too much on my mother.

I didn't speak Japanese and couldn't tell up from down as far as ingredients were concerned. Mom rattled off the words *gobo, goma, dashi, daikon, namasu,* and *nappa* [burdock root, sesame seeds, soup stock, Japanese white radish, vinegared seasoned raw fish, and vegetable greens] as easily as I could recite the words bubble gum, lollipop, potato chips, and cola. But what would I do when I left home? I would be lost.

I might, if lucky, be able to recognize some items in an Asian grocery store. With that realization I decided to act. During my last months of living at home, I started asking Mom for recipes. I had been a county fair blue-ribbon-winning baker; I'd taken 4-H baking classes and claimed a good inch-thick stack of award ribbons for my cookies and cupcakes. I was used to getting traditional step-by-step, thoroughly written instructions. Documenting my mother's recipes proved most challenging.

My mom was a great cook. I think she cooked by gestalt, tossing in ingredients she'd been familiar with for decades. Repetition and memory dissolved a need to follow printed words on paper. Cooking was ingrained within her: a spoonful of sugar here, a dollop of minced ginger there. At the same time, she maintained high standards. I remember her splashing liquids into some dishes—tasting, adding sugar, wine or water, tasting again—until she was satisfied it was just right. She could be her own best critic.

"Tasty teriyaki chicken, Masa!" my Uncle Ben would say at our New Year's celebration. She might blush or laugh, then add softly, "Thank you, but I think it's a little *karai* [salty]. Just a little more sugar and less soy sauce would have been better."

It was perfect, Mom, really.

Mom hardly measured. When I asked her how much sugar and salt and vinegar she used for the sushi dressing for the rice, she'd say something like: "You add about a cup of sugar and enough vinegar so that it is not too sour." She'd squint her eyes and pucker her lips to the side. How could I interpret that? For me, vinegar in any amount was always sour.

I struggled with transcribing her instructions into words on paper. I dealt with this: soak two heaping scoops of dry rice submerged in water that is up to the line of your first knuckle. In a saucepan over low heat, melt some sugar into vinegar. Set aside. Cook the rice. When done, add the melted sugar and vinegar dressing and mix until rice kernels are glossy. Constantly fan the cooling rice as you mix. The vinegar will evaporate as the mixture cools, and you add just enough dressing to the rice until you get a slightly stronger degree of flavor for your finished sushi than you want at the end.

Off and on throughout the years I experimented, trying to perfect a re-creation of my mother's sushi recipe. Sometimes there was too much liquid and the rice was mushy; other times the rice, cooked with too little water, turned dry and crunchy. After adding and subtracting amounts and comparing them with other sushi recipes I had found in cookbooks, I concocted a list of ingredients and instructions that asked for oddball measurements like this: 5/8 cup rice vinegar to 2.65 cups cooked dry rice. When I thought I had finally gotten it right, much to my pleasure as well as my mother's, I sat at the dining table with my parents and a plateful of my not-so-well-rolled morsels of cut sushi in front of us. I was hoping the basic proportions of rice and water and vinegar and sugar would be duplicated to her satisfaction. A fully seeped delicate taste, the correct texture—that's what I really wanted. I waited.

I asked, "Is it how it is supposed to be?"

There is momentary silence. She and Dad are chewing. Finally, someone speaks.

"Yes, this is really good, Brenda," Mom answered. My dad nodded in agreement.

My heart somersaulted. I had gotten it right! To this day, I still use Mom's recipe. It is how I can be with her again. Sometimes I've cut back on the sugar or salt, trying to cook more health consciously, cutting down on sweets and those things we are told are bad for us. Mom's recipe is sweeter than what you find in restaurants. But if I altered my original template, fiddled with the vinegar and sugar brine, and tried to dilute it in the rice, my dad always commented.

"Is it different this time?" he asked.

"Well...yes, I put in less sugar and vinegar...umm trying to be ...." I needn't say more. Already, I knew I had failed in his eyes.

It wasn't until a few years ago while reading a Japanese cookbook given to me for my birthday that I learned the sweetness of sushi varies traditionally according to the regions of Japan in which it is cooked. The preference of stronger sugar content of sushi gradually increases as one progresses south. My grandparents were from Hiroshima, and this may have been one of the reasons my family made a sweeter version of sushi.

Once I learned how to make the sushi rice, I still had to perfect the art of rolling it onto a flat square of *nori* [dried seaweed processed into thin sheets]. Mom had taught me how to layer the rice on top of the nori with cooked, dried gourd strips, pickled ginger, scrambled egg, sliced carrots, and shiitake mushroom. Cooking these ingredients often took hours because I used the same broth for the mushrooms, the dried gourd, and the carrots. Mom rolled her sushi rice perfectly: little colorful bits of filling surrounded by a symmetrical layer of rice and nori.

"Try to get the red, pickled ginger in the center of the roll— like a bull's-eye," she would coach me. My practice sushi always seemed to come out lopsided or skewed to one side. We handled the most expensive ingredient, broiled eel from Japan marinated in a rich sugar and soy sauce, with the utmost respect. It dotted the inner sanctum of the sushi roll.

Exit eel and enter carp.

BRENDA NAKAMOTO

FISH

The water in the canal departed from the river a half-mile to the north, at first running parallel to the banks of the Feather River before diverging towards a different direction of the valley. Through a line of tall cottonwoods and oaks, river beckoned, laying in her path a wide swath of green down the valley. Water in perpetual motion, fed by the Sierra snowpack and spring runoff—unchecked in winter fury of flood-churned boulders and whitewater, and swollen and frothy in the glassy calm of summer—swept through the banks of this river that meandered through the landscape.

My cousins Rodney and Glen took me fishing at the canal by their house; it was my first time at the sport. This canal was about fifteen feet wide and bordered by levees of soil rolling like little hilly ridges on each side. The greenish brown water running within these banks would irrigate crops in Butte and Sutter Counties. Along with the water came fish and plants and arthropods. Aquatic leafy vegetation floated on top, scratching the smooth surface; the canal smelled dank with clams and aquatic life. We fashioned poles out of long peach tree limbs found lying in the orchard. Rodney secured a fishing line with a hook and a weight to one end. We skewered small pieces of bologna to the hooks, tossed in our lines, and waited. Almost immediately, my cousins were catching fish. "Jerk it!" Rodney yelled.

My reactions were slow, and by the time I pulled the line out of the water, the bologna would be gone. Rodney and Glen instructed me to watch the end of the pole, look for movement, feel the nibble. I couldn't feel anything except the current pulling on my line and sinker. Then I felt something, something like a knocking at a door. This time, I tugged quickly. That is what I was told to do; it would make the hook dig into the fish's mouth.

"I got one!"

I had a fish struggling on my line, a small carp, dangling from my makeshift fishing pole. I pulled it out of the canal and placed it in a bucket of water already brimming with others my cousins had caught. Eventually, we took the bucket frothing with lively activity back to their house and emptied it into a big laundry tub filled with water. But when fish started going belly up heaving their gills gasping for breath, we felt sorry for them and carried them back to the canal and tossed them back in. Most of them disappeared into the depths of the water, but my fish, the little carp, wouldn't swim. It continued to float belly up. I watched the carp getting pulled in the current until it reached the weir. It lingered at the brim of the uppermost board. Swim, little fish. My eyes followed it until its silver image disappeared lifeless over the edge. It was then that the gravity of my situation hit me. I could not reverse something to the way it was before; I had taken away life from the river.

In late fall and winter, the flow in the canal slowed. With no need to deliver water to crops, the water-district ditch tender closed the entry gates from the Feather River, and the canal gradually dried up. Rodney and I walked the levees, watching the receding green waters of the canal. The waterline barely dipped at first, but then the smooth, slick wall of mud of the exposed bank lengthened below the line of grass topping the levee above. By mid-winter, with the water almost completely drained, there were but puddles remaining, miniature lakes in the bottom of the canal trough. Silver fins and silver sides flashed in the foot-deep water. Fish thrashed and splashed, trying to escape imminent death.

"Can't we gather them in buckets and take them back to the river? We can carry them on our bikes." I knew it would be futile, but I had to ask.

Rodney shook his head. We crept down the sides of the bank towards the water. It was steep and slippery. I grabbed at clumps of Johnson grass—that sturdy, razor-sharp weed disdained by farmers—to slow my descent, then let go and ran and slipped crazily towards the bottom. Rodney was waiting for me, assessing the situation. He skipped rocks in the puddles and poked his fingers in mud. The empty shells of Asian clams lined the clay. Animal tracks crisscrossed in trails around the water's edge. Probably coyotes and raccoons feasted during this time, though, I didn't see anything, only fish circling. I heard that people would sneak into these canals and gig trout and suckers and carp. This time the place gave me the creeps and there was nothing I could do. Again, I thought about the current of life that ran through here, about our river that had been like an artery pumping blood through the valley. I bundled into my jacket and gingerly climbed out of the canal. How different this was compared to summer. All the splashy, hot-weather fun from a little while ago now felt like an illusion.

This is how my mind has worked—okazu, goulash, fish, sushi—all so different and yet in some ways much the same. See how it has twisted and turned, just like that canal and river did, snaking their way through the valley.

MAKI ZUSHI

Masa Nakamoto's Recipe

GLOSSARY OF TERMS

Dashi is soup stock. This recipe calls for dried bonito soup stock that is sold in powder form and reconstituted with water to make dashi.

Kampyo are dried gourd strips.

Dried *shiitake* mushrooms can be found at Asian markets in various sizes.

Unagi is eel. Grilled eel from Japan is cooked in a sweet sauce and sold in cans or cellophane packages.

Maki zushi is a sheet of nori rolled over rice and fillings.

Nori is seaweed dried and processed into squares of thin, flat sheets.

Rice paddle, used to fluff rice

Bamboo mat, used to roll rice and fillings together

Short-grain rice is used for making sushi

INGREDIENTS

1 package kampyo
8 dried shiitake mushrooms
1 carrot
$\frac{1}{2}$ teaspoon cornstarch
2 eggs
1 tablespoon cooking oil
1 can or package of grilled unagi
6 cups water
3 tablespoons dried bonito soup stock
$\frac{1}{4}$ cup soy sauce
$\frac{1}{4}$ cup sugar
$\frac{5}{8}$ cup rice vinegar
$\frac{1}{2}$ cup sugar
1 teaspoon salt
1 tablespoon sake
2 $\frac{3}{4}$ cup dry short-grain white rice
3 $\frac{1}{4}$ cups water
7-10 sheets nori
$\frac{1}{4}$ cup sliced pickled ginger

rice paddle
bamboo mat

1. In a bowl, cover kampyo and dried shiitake mushrooms in water and soak for several hours. Drain and set aside.
2. Peel and slice carrot into ¼-inch lengthwise strips
3. In a small bowl, mix ½ teaspoon cornstarch with ½ teaspoon water, 2 eggs, and a dash of soy sauce and salt. Beat together until frothy. Meanwhile, heat a frying pan to medium temperature. Coat bottom of pan with a tablespoon of cooking oil. Pour in egg mixture. Fry until bottom of egg pancake is lightly browned and set. Flip and cook another minute. Remove and place on cutting board. Slice into ½-inch strips.
4. Grilled unagi from Japan is precooked in a sweet sauce. Follow instructions on the package of unagi that you have purchased. There may be no need for additional cooking except to toast and warm the ingredients in the oven before use. Slice unagi in ⅜-inch lengthwise strips. Set aside.
5. Combine the 6 cups water, dried bonito soup stock, soy sauce, and sugar in a stock pot. Add soaked kampyo and shiitake mushrooms and bring to a boil. Simmer kampyo for 15 minutes until tender, then remove from the broth and drain in a colander. Continue to cook the shiitake mushrooms for a total of 30 minutes, then remove from broth. Remove stems from mushrooms and discard; slice mushroom caps into ⅜-inch-wide strips. Add carrot strips to broth and cook until tender but firm, about 15 minutes.
6. To make the vinegar and sugar dressing, in a small saucepan, heat vinegar and sugar over medium heat. Stir until sugar melts and mixture starts to boil. Add salt and sake. Set aside and cool.
7. Rinse rice in pot until water runs clear. Soak rice in water for 30 minutes. On stove over high heat, bring the rice mixture to a boil, cover pot with a lid, lower to medium heat, and simmer for 25 minutes. Do not open lid.
8. Empty cooked rice from pot into a bowl. Pour the vinegar and sugar dressing over the rice. Fluff rice with a rice paddle, using gentle, cutting strokes, separating the kernels and evenly coating them with the dressing. With a free

hand or the assistance of a helper, fan the rice mixture briefly. Do not overmix or mash grains. Cover bowl with a paper towel dampened in water. Set aside.

9. Heat a stove burner to medium heat. Wave a sheet of nori over the burner to toast it for a few seconds, until the color changes to a deeper green. Do this to the remaining sheets.

10. Set aside pickled ginger on a kitchen counter or at a table where you want to start rolling sushi. Place the other prepared ingredients there, also: kampyo, mushrooms, carrots, eggs, unagi, rice and nori.

11. To roll the maki zushi, put one sheet of nori on top of a bamboo mat. Gently coat the sheet of nori with a $\frac{3}{8}$-inch layer of rice, leaving about an inch of the nori sheet that is farthest from you sprinkled with just a few grains of rice. On the side nearest you and about an inch from the edge, layer in a line from left to right a few strips of kampyo, mushrooms, carrots, unagi, pickled ginger, and egg. With the aid of the bamboo mat, carefully begin rolling nori, rice and fillings into a cylinder. As you roll forward and press ingredients together, curl back the edges of the bamboo mat until the nori and rice are completely enclosed around the center of the filling. Apply steady pressure to the bamboo mat to tamp the ingredients together, creating a tight roll. Open mat and pat ends of roll between hands. You have now successfully made one maki zushi!

Continue assembling the ingredients together with the rice as described above. This recipe makes about 8 rolls. Just before the meal, with a wet knife, slice rolls into 1 $\frac{1}{4}$-inch pieces.

Arrange onto a decorative platter and enjoy.

BRENDA NAKAMOTO

MOCHI

"Mochi!" my kids squeal, bursting through the front door, eying a shallow box of Japanese confection set atop a footstool. Off falls the ribbon and white wrapping paper.

"Mochi!" they shout. They flip open the lid, exposing twelve pressed mounds of cooked rice balls lining the inside of the box like chicken eggs.

"I want pink," says Noriko.

"I get green," yelps Toshi.

I sneak one that's white and bite before anyone notices. It is just before dinner.

We love mochi. Our enthusiasm must be hard to comprehend for the non-Japanese, because this food takes some getting used to. Made of steamed rice pounded and molded over a center of sweetened bean paste, mochi is mushy and sticky, the texture chewy. Each one is dense and heavy enough to be pitched like a baseball; my eleven-year-old Little Leaguer might hit a nice pop fly with one.

And it bounces against the fence! Toshi bats in a run!

The last bit of a mochi disappears into my mouth. I wipe my cornstarch-dusted lips before greeting my husband, who had obviously purchased our treats and left them for us to find. I give him a hug. He is so thoughtful. How he understands the pleasure I get from this food, my soul food! Mochi and I share a long history.

There is much more to mochi than this fistful of rice in my hands. In fact, this food harkens to much earlier times.

Rice was considered sacred in ancestral Japan. Not only providing a source of sustenance, it was also offered as gifts to the gods. According to Shinto tradition, a *tamashii*, a spirit, resided in each grain of rice; thus, mochi cakes formed of pounded, glutinous rice represented the combination of millions of souls. These spirits visited during the winter holidays, and *mochitsuki*, traditional mochi-making ceremonies, were held throughout Japanese communities. A wooden mallet struck repetitively onto hot, steaming rice in a stone or wooden mortar transformed simple rice into that of a delicacy.

Heave, ho, huff, puff and go!

A big wooden mallet hits the dough
hot, steamed rice, sweet and sticky,

pearly white and a little bit tricky
One man pummels while the other one turns

Heave, ho, huff, puff and go!

Oh rice grain, moist and glossy, white and steamy
for such an apparent innocence,
such a dramatic conversion to a oneness
Mochi cakes rise; fulfill your destiny
Heave, ho, huff, puff and go!

What energy! What celebration! As a child, I remember waiting for Mom and Dad to come home from the church mochitsuki. Mom had gabbed all day with her women friends while shaping rice patties, and Dad and the men wrestled with rice pounding and church cleanup. They walked in the house dusted with powdery white cornstarch on their clothes and their arms carrying bags filled with mochi. The fresh cakes were soft and warm. I often devoured some at that moment.

There was no waiting for me.

Just before the New Year, Mom stacked two mochi on top of

each other and topped them with a tangerine. This was our offering to the Amida Buddha placed in front of the shrine on top of the bedroom dresser. Baachan lit sticks of incense and set them in sand in a tiny, bronze bowl. Fragrant smoke twisted upwards in thin lines. The smell of forest and musk seeped through the walls of our house, awakening a sense in me of something new, unearthly. During this holiday period, my baachan's room transformed into something sacred. It brought me to a place that extended well beyond the edges of her bed and walls. The black and white photos of my relatives long since passed from this earth looked back at me out of tarnished picture frames. I would examine their faces recorded on a grainy film and think, "Thank you, I will remember you." These were tangible actions, and I thought by doing so, a part of me was linked to the spirits of my ancestors.

On New Year's Eve, Mom and I stayed awake until midnight, glued to the television set, watching the countdown at New York's Times Square where a bobbing sea of people bundled in coats and hats stood under a wave of floating confetti. The clock had counted down to zero; and then magically it was officially New Year's Day, and Mom and I joined in to singing "Auld Lang Syne."

Should auld acquaintance be forgot,
and never brought to mind?
Should auld acquaintance be forgot,
and auld lang syne?

"More mochi!" we chimed around the dining table, early on New Year's Day when we fished out chewy blobs of cooked rice cakes from bottoms of bowls. Ladled from a big pot of hot clam broth, blander than a dumpling and stickier than chewing gum, melted mochi stretched into long strings between my mouth and chopsticks.

"Don't play with your food," Mom scolded.

I'd twirl the gooey blob around my finger, watch it drip and droop like honey. First, drink all the clam broth from the bowl, then with the remaining mochi patty stuck at the bottom, douse it proportionally in sugar and soy sauce. Delicious.

Mom limited how much we could eat and maintained that one mochi was equal to a bowl of rice. She said a man once ate so much mochi he was hospitalized and had his stomach pumped. What a price to pay for such indulgence! No matter. That didn't stop me.

I cradle a mochi in my right hand, a baseball mitt on the left. I lift a foot, rock back, pitch overhand, watch the mochi spin slow motion towards my son. His eyes alight at the oncoming projectile. He swings—Whump!—and bat and mochi meet.

Mochi flies over second base, over center field. It is gone, gone, gone! Like a shooting star, it streaks across the horizon, bursts through the heavens, driving towards the moon.

Some of my mother's traditions faded with her passing, for I am not as observant of the nuances of Japanese ritual and ceremony as she was. My mother took great care in raising me so that customs were properly followed: why there were particular Japanese words spoken, foods cooked for certain occasions, why we wore what we did when we went to church. With her death, a part of me also left, a part that was unknowingly tied to Japan. Later I accepted that I was who I was, the scariest part was living with this uncertainty without her.

I believe in tamashii, that there might be rebirth, a life force sprung forth once again after death. That spirit is me; that spirit is us.

Rice. I love rice. I like it steamed and sticky, I like it salted and boiled. I like it pounded and shaped into balls. Without rice, I would not be here, that is certain. Rice grains, we tamashii, are bound together.

After the winter holidays were over, Baachan removed our offerings from the dresser, the dried-out and cracked mochi cakes now zig-zagged with a crust looking like that of old paint. She chopped and broke these chunks of rice into small pieces and dropped them into a hot cast-iron pan under a tight-fitting lid. Within this incubator, the cakes steamed and warmed again into something soft and pliable, smelling of popcorn, toasted on the outside and hot and moist on the inside. With a little attention they had been rejuvenated, revitalized with new life. Then Baachan and I dipped them in sugar and devoured. Ummm.

BRENDA NAKAMOTO

FIRE

Daddy stands in front of a fire, golden flames aglow behind him, tree branches and trunks whistling and crackling in heat against the carmine horizon of the fading evening sunset above the Sutter Buttes. Air reeks with burning gasoline and tar from rubber tires scattered about the base of trees bulldozed and piled together. Bright flames flicker through unspent fuel and glow incandescent at opposite sides of the clearing where the Carolyn peach trees once stood, where only a few months earlier had arched brittle branches covered in ripe fruits, crippled, aged, and bent upon crutches for support at their last harvest. The limbs had been reinforced by one-by-fours forked at the top and stuck upright in the ground, in a forest of wooden props. And now, in the dead of winter, this tree variety was gone, stacked in a tangle of bark and roots, two horses high and two horses wide. Daddy watches the burning wood with hands on his hips, eyes and face and shirt layered in soot. His skin is blackened, doused with the swirl of putrid smoke that circles around him. He doesn't notice us and shakes his head.

Daddy has tended the woodpiles all day, feeding them, loading unspent fuel on top with the tractor and brush rake to stoke the flames. The forks of the rake he had crafted himself, welded out of six-inch plumbing pipe that he affixed to the front of the tractor. He plunges the brush rake into the fire, lifting up the burning limbs and stirring them in the pile. The tractor moans and squeals when the hydraulic fork raises limbs high in the air. Daddy at the helm pushes forward and back, working the fire as if corralling farm animals, compacting a limb here, lifting a snapping log there. Around the edges of the firestorm, the winter soil is pulverized and powdered with burnt carbon. The fire burns hot.

I stand a safe distance away, the spitting, hissing, and popping sounds of the wood resins intermixing with the quiet calm of the cool night air. Daddy jumps off the tractor and stays close to the flames. He stares into the fire with wild eyes and eyeglasses that reflect the flashes and shadows of sizzling wood. He turns and paces while the black smoke billows.

Mommy brings Daddy bentoo: a few rice balls and marinated meat and pickled vegetables on a foil-covered paper plate. She's added a canning jar filled with creamed and sugared coffee. He nods and smiles with tired eyes when he sees us, backs away from the flames to greet us and get his meal.

I had forgotten the marshmallows. If I had brought them, I could have skewered them onto the ends of long peach branches and toasted them to a caramel brown above the warmed, charred wood.

The tree roots reach towards me, stretch to the sky with tentacles clinging to particles of earth. They say goodbye.

At midnight, Daddy comes home, stinking up the house with a burnt smell. He lays his sooty shirt, pants and boots on the floor and traipses to the bathroom in boxer shorts, his white legs and white torso in stark contrast to blackened face and arms dusted in carbon. The burnt smell follows him wherever he goes, and soon the stench trails from laundry hamper, down the hall and to the shower. After he washes with shampoo and soap and scrubs his fingernails and hair getting out the particles of fire, the smoke smell lingers on his body and on his wash and bath towels. Long afterwards, his clothes will still retain the remnants of fire, until Mom scrubs them with detergent on the accordion-warped washboard and tosses them in the washing machine.

Some things want to cling to existence. Some things try to stay the way they are. And trees and orchards long gone and burnt to powder come up and out of nowhere to mix again with life.

BRENDA NAKAMOTO

FIRE, AIR, AND SMOKE

People gather in that room lined with pews coursing down the aisle one after the other. Footsteps tread lightly on carpet and voices whisper in the quiet. Be careful; others are watching. Overhead, a dragon glares on the crowd below, the same dragon painted decades earlier, the one who stood guard over Sunday school sermons, weddings, funerals, and holiday services. He pranced in a timeless pose with foot raised, mouth opened, and teeth bared. And even though the gilded paint has faded and the once-vivid oranges and yellows and reds are dulled, the creature frozen on the wall still casts a ferocious snarl from above.

That same image graces the bronze pot of incense set at the head of the pews in front of the altar. Smoke rises in stair-step circles through the nose of the bronze dragon, lingering together in a gray cloud below the ceiling. Fire, air, and smoke: these are things of nature, these are things of which the world is made.

"Sit down, cross your legs. Be quiet," Mom would whisper in hushed tones. "Don't fiddle with your *ojuzu* [meditation beads]. The strand may break. Shhh!"

Mom was the one who quietly directed orders, who behind the scenes told us how to stand, sit, walk, or bow. Family looked to her for proper etiquette, because this was a temple and a social function, and customs were to be followed. Yet, this time, there is something different, something people aren't used to. The members in the front right pews bow their heads in silence. Black suits, black dresses, and permed hairdos. Something is wrong; someone is missing. Mom is not here. She is up front, lying in a coffin. With her face powdered, lips glossed, and the smoke from burning incense clouded above her, she looks like she's sleeping.

In the raised altar just behind her sits Reverend Aoyama.

From the side and hidden behind a curtain, he pounds several times on the temple bell and begins chanting. Candles flicker, the flaming tips wavering on the candelabras next to the painting of the Amida Buddha. The golden altar glows. The reverend hums an incantation and the sounds of his verse emanate from deep within, oozing out in volume. It flows out slowly; it rises and recedes.

Soo ohh ohh oh-oh-oh *mmmmmmmm*
Soo ohh ohh oh-oh-oh mmmmmmmmmm
bong bong bonnnnnnnng

Ooh ooh ooohhhhh mmmmm
bong-bong-bonnng

Mom would approve of the seating arrangement. Dad is up in the front pew near her feet. There is Carol, the eldest daughter, with her husband and child, Arlene with her husband and two boys, and then there's me, the youngest. Mom would notice that the flowers are arranged properly. Dad's giant wreath of carnations leans majestically against an easel. It is the biggest, the prettiest, and the most prominent. Smaller circles of wreaths follow to the side, ducklings waddling after their mother. Love Carol and family. Love Arlene and family. The last wreath is from me. Love Brenda. It is the littlest, the most modest. That is proper. That is its place. I am always last.

It wasn't so long ago when Mom and Dad were in the front seat of the car, that old, purple 1970s Oldsmobile cruiser, driving back home from a funeral at this very same church, and she and he were whispering to each other in voices low so that children couldn't eavesdrop.

"Did you see how Sachiyo was dressed? One is not supposed to be in colors. And why is Emi still wearing those same old rags? Makes it so that I can't even buy a new dress!"

Her voice drifts back, wavers in the room, speaking to no one, catching the attention of this one onlooker in the second pew: me. Now, not bound by rules, she chatters unpredictably, tapping at the walls and rustling through the folds of velvet curtains. I listen, reaching for memories.

Keep talking, Mommy. I can hear you.

I CANNOT, NOT YET

I knock on the door of my dad's apartment at Covell Gardens, an assisted-living complex for seniors here in Davis. There is no answer, yet I can hear his grunts and mumblings, and I open the door slightly.

"Hi, Dad!" I say. He putters about the room, hobbling dangerously to each side as he shuffles across the floor. He walks near the walls and positions himself a few steps from a chair and a table, his outstretched hands leading him forward.

"Hi, Dad!" I say again. This time I shout.

"Ah!" He jerks his shoulders and teeters, then grips onto the rubber handles of the walker that help him balance. He recognizes me and relaxes.

He says, "I can't find my gloves. They were right here in my basket; this morning they are gone. I think one of the housekeepers must have stolen them. Things are always missing and someone takes my things in the middle of the night!"

I rummage through the contents of a bag that is attached to the walker. It is made of muslin and stained with drips of juice. One of the ladies at the complex donated it to a garage sale three years ago and Dad bought it for twenty-five cents. With clips and rings and duct tape, he hooked it onto the tubes of his walker. I open this bag and rummage inside its contents. I find bundles of napkins and zip-lock bags bound together with rubber bands, the remnants of a sugar cookie, a hardened muffin, one grapefruit, a baseball hat, and then something soft and furry stuffed at the bottom.

"Here they are," I say, pulling a pair of knit gloves from the bag. "I'm ready to take you to Walmart."

BRENDA NAKAMOTO

Walmart has become a place I travel to frequently, now that Dad lives in the same town as me. With all the medications he needs for glaucoma, dry eyes, eczema, and high blood pressure, Dad shops frequently at this discount store for the senior on a fixed budget. He can get more for less. So off I go, leading Dad out the apartment door and down the main hallway. Personally, I hate Walmart. I don't hate it, exactly, it's just that on weekends, I'd rather be anywhere else than in a packed warehouse-sized building, fighting my way through crowds and dodging a shopping cart past kids who dart between the aisles. I will be a cow mooing my way through the store, and I will be dutiful daughter following in her father's footsteps. No, this time I will be leading his footsteps.

His breathing quickens as he follows me down the carpeted hallway of the assisted-living complex. He labors as he walks, "Ah, ah, oh, oh, ah, ah, ahhhh." He can't hear himself; one of his ears is deaf from surgery to remove a benign tumor in his head, and now, even the other good ear can't hear much either.

"How are you?" I ask him.

"What's new?" he asks me. He misinterprets, looks at me with rheumy eyes swollen with eye drops and lubricants. "Oh, nothing's new. Gawd, I have to get out. There're too many old people around here."

I ignore that he didn't hear my question. Close enough. I watch him struggle to push that metal walker across the floor, that four-wheeled contraption with a high-tech braking system, a basket and a seat. It's a second home on wheels. I can't help but remember when he wasn't this way.

Back in his heyday, my father was tough and snappy, quick with calculations, a spitfire. He bought his first twenty-five-acre parcel of land from savings accumulated after serving four years in the U.S. Army during WWII. He had been a cook in the Military Intelligence Service, which was responsible for holding Japanese prisoners of war in Australia. During his years of service, Dad squirreled away $1,200 from his military allowance. He used it to pay in full the balance for the title to an apricot orchard owned by a Caucasian woman. He said her husband had died, and that was why she was selling. Dad was drafted and wasn't able to purchase the land at the time, but she said she would hold the property for him, as he had been making installments. When Dad was discharged and returned to California, however, he almost wasn't able to acquire the land. The owner had changed her mind. But Dad was lucky, because she kept her word and sold it to him.

He told me that when he first farmed the piece, he lived in his pickup truck because there was no house on the parcel. He ran the irrigation water through the orchard, a process that lasted many days from start to finish, and he cooked his meals on a camp stove and slept at nights in the bed of the truck. In his forties and fifties, my dad had skin tanned a permanent brown, in a v-shape shadow about his neck. He was one tough man who yelled out of necessity, I guess, and we all followed his orders. A farm demanded year-round care: thinning after the set of fruit, spraying for pests, plowing to control weeds. And, of course, there was that extra stressful three-month period of time at harvest during summer when Dad and Mom, my uncle and aunt, and all us six kids from both families had everything on the line: our whole year's work or, for that matter, our whole life's savings tottering in that period. It was a time of fruition, of accomplishment. Peaches converted to money for paying bills and debt, and with luck, a little extra.

I position the walker next to the car and help Dad get into the passenger seat. It takes him extra effort to bend down and to move his feet underneath the dash. I turn on the engine and we are skimming north on Highway 113 to Woodland. Alongside the road are fields fallowed for winter and red-tailed hawks perched on telephone poles. The car fills with a sickly, sweet odor and it's hard for me to take a breath without feeling like retching. Dad smells bad. We had talked about hygiene before, but I think now it's gotten worse. He's a leaky faucet with a worn washer that can't be replaced, and he doesn't even notice. I wish I could talk further about this. Somehow I can't muster the courage. No, I cannot tell him. I roll down the window and let in the cold winter air. It only dilutes the problem. It is still there.

My mother had told us three daughters after she and Dad were retiring from farming that she and he were going to be free people—they would no longer be slaves to the land. I remember her announcing they had suffered enough, suffered taking care of the trees and us kids. Now they would finally have fun and enjoy themselves.

"Don't expect any babysitting," she had said. I was single at the time and didn't really mind the comment, but I couldn't help but think, "How could they just abandon us?"

Mom and Dad did what they said; they started enjoying life. Mom bought fancy, frilly dresses, things she had never owned before as a farmer's wife. My old bedroom became a closet where skirts and blouses and dresses lined the floor under a handmade clothes rack my dad engineered out of plumbing pipe. Dad twirled and whirled my mother in the foxtrot, the tango, the jitterbug, and other dance steps they had mastered. They turned into accomplished swing dancers, and I must say I was impressed when I watched them tapping their feet to the tunes blaring from live brass bands, holding hands and looking at each other as if they'd never seen one another before. Their happiness was the beginning of a new era for them. My mother, true to form, spent their money and dragged my father on trips to Sweden, Norway, Alaska, Washington DC, Florida, Russia and Japan. Then, Mom passed out on the floor after a dance and died from heart failure.

I feel the cool air swim around my face, dispelling the memory of her. Mom went out doing what she loved in this world—

dancing with Dad. I hear him mumble to himself beside me. My two young kids argue in the backseat; they know how to work me. They know I'm an easy squeeze for buying things. If Mom were here, she would tell me I am spoiling them, giving them too much.

I can't tell if it would be easier to go out quickly like she did or to just stumble along like my dad. It's hard for him. It's hard for me. In the years since her death I've watched Dad age. First, he wanted to die, to kill himself so that he could be with Mom. But he got over that, made new friends, and continued the life of a dancer. Some years later, bacteria invaded his prosthetic knee, and he was hospitalized. Doctors removed the infected prosthetic, and Dad recuperated for six weeks on intravenous antibiotics. The femur and tibia were temporarily screwed together and we waited for the infection to clear; Dad hobbled about with that leg stiff like a pirate's peg. The infection had almost cost him his life; but I don't think that he ever realized the severity of his condition, because that never stopped his complaints. He didn't like his recovery in the convalescent hospital; he didn't like the nurses, he argued with the doctors. My dad was still my same dad: a spitfire. Yet I have tried to put myself in his place, immobile, without his lifetime love, and I saw him in a new light, in a way I have never seen before.

"I'm going to walk again. I want out of this place," he'd say, looking at the man in the bed next to him—the man with a vacant expression, the one who never smiled or talked. My dad faced this stage of his life alone, and I remember walking into the convalescent hospital room hearing him reciting his prayers. "Dear God, please bless Masa, Baachan, Sumi, Bob and Chi. Thank them for sharing their lives with me. Watch over them." He eventually underwent surgery for a second prosthetic knee. He walked again, and he left the convalescent hospital and moved into Covell Gardens.

While I am noticing my kids are learning new things in school, I am watching my father losing things, facing hardships in

BRENDA NAKAMOTO

his later years. I remember that Dad had overcome poverty, built a modest farming business, then retired with a pot of money bigger than he could have ever dreamed of as a child. Now he sits here an older man, outliving my mother by many years. He should be proud that he took care of things the way he did: raising three daughters who grew up to be contributing members of society, providing for the whims of my mother, and making a living in an America just getting used to the idea of equality amongst people of color. When I look at him, I sometimes feel at a loss because he is less than what I remember. I know it is unfair to judge him. I wrestle with how I feel and how I should feel. There is an overriding factor that intervenes. Dad, you've earned your stripes. You earned them in the army, you earned them on the farm, and you earned them with me.

I roll up the window of the car, shutting out the brisk air that encloses me in thoughts that I feel but can never voice.

Harold Nakamoto's invention
for wiring peach trees

BRENDA NAKAMOTO

STRINGING WIRE

I finger the edges of a faded black and white photo found buried in the filing cabinet, one of the few remaining documents of life on our family farm. Mom is gone, the orchards and property are sold; many decades have passed, and little is left of my agricultural past except wayward memories. I look closely at the photo. My fingers pause over this artifact. My eight-year-old daughter Noriko had plucked it from the files and given it to my sister Carol, who had given it to me. All of us daughters were in Daddy's apartment, cleaning before moving him to a higher level of care at the assisted-living facility.

"I found it, Mommy. What is it?" my daughter had asked.

"Oh, really?" I answered, my thoughts elsewhere. Yet, I had not realized what a treasure she had found until I examined closer. Something from afar called to me.

Carol doesn't remember, doesn't recollect having a purpose for this peculiar photo; although, I argue the handwriting on the back scrawled in cursive—*Daddy's invention 1967*—is certainly hers. There's the old shed in the background, with wide, sliding, sheet metal doors that he had welded and bolted together. They hung from six-inch rollers that moved on a rail, opening and closing the entrances to the shed that stored our tractors, trucks, and trailer.

My eyes stare and focus; and within the time of my long gaze, things start to animate, blossoming into life and movement. Within that photo, an old automobile tire axle converted to the function of a spool is mounted at the base of an iron mesh platform elevated above a tractor. The spool spins outward like a fishing reel, whirling wire at the treetops alongside a young Daddy, who maneuvers with outstretched hands. He is standing next to a bundle of wire, gloves on his hands, as wire slides between his fingertips, ten feet off the ground with just enough room to stand and to take a few steps in each direction. Like a sewing bobbin, the axle rotates, coincident with the movement of the tractor below with Uncle Bob driving at the wheel; both he and Daddy are together, circling around each peach tree so that wire can be strung in the uppermost branches.

"Hup!" my dad shouts, and raises a hand.

Uncle Bob halts the tractor, stands up and hands an extra pair of pliers to my dad. Two brothers appear side by side, one on top—that is my father—and my uncle a few feet below, straddling the tractor seat in his boots, both of them stair-stepping each other at an angle, looking so much alike they could be mistaken for twins. My father, the older and slightly smaller one, is hidden under a knit hat and down-filled parka. Uncle Bob is the huskier one in similar clothing, a jacket differing slightly in color. Both are bundled against the cold, their puffy outlines from layers of clothing like that of the Pillsbury Doughboy. Time is altered when I gaze into the photo. I see steam puffing from the brothers' lips when they exchange words in the icy winter air. There is turquoise sky and bare tree limbs and frost covering the ground.

"Go ahead!" my dad directs.

My uncle nods, sits on the tractor seat cushion, and with his left foot stamps down on the clutch and grinds the iron rod of the transmission between his legs into first, the engine mumbles and groans. He moves the machinery forward: the tractor, the wire spindle, the platform, and my dad swaying on top of the welded invention.

A biting wind races through cirrus-laced winter sky, combing the wispy clouds stacked against the peaks of the Sierras to the east. Woolen hats and gloves bend submissively in the cold air that seeps between the woof and warp of fabric. Up high and exposed in the treetops, my father works. He casts out wire around a tree, wraps it snugly about the high branches. He secures the ends, mashing them with the pliers, looping and cutting and twisting together unfinished ends, forming a continuous ring of metal at the uppermost boughs. Sometimes he inserts a washer in the center of the circle, runs wire crisscross through the hole, angling them together through a central hub at the treetop. This spider's web, he says, supports the limbs when they are laden with ripe fruit.

Dad cinches tightly the ring of wire, the invisible backbone of the tree, when in summer cling peaches will weigh heavily on the canopy branches. The two brothers hope to harvest almost a half-ton of fruit from each tree. They depend on this enigmatic ring. Bond between farmer and tree and wire age together: tree needing wire to prop its branches, farmer depending on fruits to finance a livelihood, and wire, inanimate object, needing nothing and giving all. Wire holds firm, girdles the tree's branches tightly. Through time the gap between tree and wire coalesces, spaces bond together, and wire and tree undergo a metamorphosis, leaving wire exposed within limbs, a thread strung through the eye of a needle.

A wind blows. It sings and whistles, touching a line, plucking a strand on a guitar. *Eeeeuuuu. EEEeeeuuu*, the wind repeats and breathes. A gust with a dangling note hangs onto the humming wire in a sustained sigh before fading away. Ring of wire calls to me, flashes back via a black and white photo.

Years pass and the old orchard expires. Gnarled trees bulldozed and uprooted, lying stacked in great pyres, burn in the middle of barren fields where flames spark and snap into the wee hours of the black night. Then wood transpires into ash and dust, leaving on the orchard floor the next morning only an empty moonscape of jagged holes and piles of powdery soot where trees once commanded the landscape. Rings of wire, however, still hold firm. A little more twisted and at odd angles hanging onto air, circles of wire now scatter throughout the spent burn piles. And orchard, once lush and green and full of spring blossoms and scent, exists only in memory.

Fires cool. Then Daddy and Uncle Bob flatten these leftover metal strands underneath their tractors. Running rubber tires over strands of wire, making them conform from sheer pressure, they knot them into manageable parcels that can be carried. Dad calls the scrap metal man, who in a big truck comes to our farm and salvages the wire bundles, hoisting them onto the truck bed and taking them away to be melted down and reshaped into other forms. Wire will undergo yet another metamorphosis.

A discarded tire axle sits idle in the farming junk pile, abandoned and emptied, until kids like Rodney and me rediscover it and jump on it and twirl like a merry-go-round. We run and grunt and push, two gawky-looking kids with scraped knees and dirt smudges on our faces and stained shirts and canvas shoes. We jump on and hold tight, our faces looking up at the dots of dizzy clouds spinning into lines of white, against blue sky striped with orchard greens and browns. Our stomachs churn in our vertigo, we laugh at these lopsided feelings. When the motion slows and shapes congeal back into flattened form, we think oh, what fun to have been thrown into another world, where lines blend together into a blurred mat, topsy-turvy. Time travels quickly, as if through decades in an instant, then stops.

Lines string past to present. Wire casts out, opening spaces between the thens and the nows. Endings and beginnings merge into a singularity.

I stare one last time at the photo, alive with these peculiar sensations. Then I blink and they stop. I've been taken there and back again, warmed by the sweet taste of hot chocolate and roasted marshmallows, the smell of burning fall leaves and the chuckle of the tractor engine. I wrap the picture, this prize, my creator of memory, in a sheet of paper and make sure the edges won't bend. I hold it close to me for a moment, then tuck it safely away in my purse and continue packing.

SPRING

STARRY NIGHT

My daughter and I walked outside last night shortly after sundown. Two bright planets suspended low in the western sky highlighted a brilliant yellow glow against the graying backdrop of the Coast Range. Just to the north, a sliver of a waxing moon hung above the horizon, barely perceptible. I stopped and thought. Was this waxing or waning? The sliver was on the right. That meant it was starting a new phase of lunar life, according to human perspective. Was it really starting anew? Wasn't it that same old moon circling around earth with the same face, the same countenance gazing at us? Beginnings and endings. They are different. They can be the same, depending on perspective.

I took Dad back to his apartment in an assisted living complex. I drove the car to the pavement outside of the reception foyer. Rising slowly to his feet, Dad grunted, oofed and ahhed, getting out of the car.

"Are you going to be okay? Can you make it home?" I asked.

"I'm fine, just get me around the corner and pointed in the right direction. I know the way to my door." He struggled with each breath, pushing the aluminum walker that he leaned onto with each step. White tennis-shoed feet moved forward in short increments. He could barely see, having fought the long-term detrimental effects of glaucoma for more than two decades. Damaged and scarred, the optic nerves weren't transmitting visual information anymore. Shadows blurred daylight to the grays of dusk, lamplight receded to the color of night. Darkness shrouded his view. With uncertainty he progressed forward. I couldn't bear to watch, thinking he might trip and fall.

"I'll push you," I volunteered. I turned him around and set

him gingerly on the walker seat. Now, I was in control and he was sitting there like a bag of groceries. I maneuvered him between the lime green walls and ivory wallpaper of this regal hallway, floating him above the olive-drab stream of carpet.

Whee! I pushed faster. The quicker I went the whiter his fingers that gripped the rubber of the walker handles, just as my infant daughter had done not so many years ago, holding onto my long hair with tight little fists that rocked within my arms. He was holding; she had been holding; I was still holding. Time had passed quickly.

Dad was much younger; I was much younger; my mom was still alive. When the orchards were in the height of ripeness, the air of the whole countryside was rich in fragrance. The smells of peaches and prunes and apples and pears and row crops perfumed the hot and muggy days and nights of summer. Farmers could think only of harvest and of getting the produce to the market. They raced, chasing time that had a firm grip about them. My dad sometimes fumed under the pressure. All within a few months, tens of thousands of dollars of produce were to be picked and hauled to the fruit-grading station and then trucked to the processing plants. Dad barked and jumped, an uneasy dog at the porch door. He was always on edge, for no one could predict the future—gusty winds, tropical storms, or hail at harvest.

I got used to losing my dad in this season, to having a part of him taken away, enslaved to a universe so unpredictable. The promissory note, that unpaid yearly loan, knocked at every farmer's door come harvest. What a pissy kind of career. But Dad didn't smoke, didn't drink, didn't do any kinds of borderline human activities to help him let off steam. He could only throw himself into working long hours—just as his own mother and father had done—and he was hard as steel wire pulled taut; he was wound up. He could sometimes even be mean. He could hold his own, though, run a tight farming business. That was my dad. And toughened and stringy and cured under the sun, my dad, a bundle of nerves and energy worked the fields at all times, day in and day out, year in and year out, so that we girls could go to grammar and high schools and to dances and football and basketball games and flirt with the boys.

Dad walked under a cloak of invisibility. I hardly saw him. He woke early—at 4 AM—and went to bed shortly after dinner. Always tending to the crops, he failed to impress my young eyes. Instead, he emerged forty years later, as a thread stretching though a floating medium, intangible strips of time, stringing the then to the now and back again. With the farm having been sold years before, I thought I lost my dad, that part who was farmer. Only one thing has held true throughout. When I am close to him, I smell the scent of his aftershave and see the slick way the hair lies atop his head, just like he used to gel it down flat when he was much younger.

In rare, stolen bits of time, Dad the farmer sometimes relaxed; he let down his guard, didn't bark at the family or at our hired hands like he would normally. The exclamations—"Bob, get over here! Bring me a ratchet,"—could be forgotten, if for just a moment. It was impossible to let go completely when everywhere turned he saw work ahead. But in one of those scant moments, when Dad was feeling spry and prankish, he took my mom and me out for a ride—not just an ordinary ride, but one on top of the hood of the pickup. We called it the jalopy, the old Chevy truck stripped bare to just the engine and chassis. No doors, no windows, only one seat, the driver's, and a pickup bed rid of everything except metal frame and two large pieces of plywood, one over the hood and one in the bed on the back. Light and maneuverable, the jalopy skipped easily across the plowed, uneven soil of the orchard floor. It was my dad's and uncle's version of a dune buggy.

BRENDA NAKAMOTO

And on one hot and starry night, when the mosquitoes were so thick I went outside in Levi 501 jeans and a long-sleeved cowboy shirt despite the stifling air, Dad had giggled like a kid and told Mom and me to lie down on the wooden platform set just above the engine. He told us to close our eyes, and he drove us away from the house. It wasn't far. Then when we opened our eyes, we could only look above us to the heaven dipping down close, black, silver, blue, big, and little spots of light streaking the sky. The Milky Way twisted and turned, mixing in with the canopy of peach leaves that blotted in and out as Dad raced the jalopy through the tree rows. Mom and I squealed in laughter, holding on for dear life, not knowing which way was north or south, up or down. It was just Dad, Mom, and me swimming in those stars and peach leaves.

I pushed my dad. With little resistance, the walker carried him. He was so light. One shove and he could float away in front of me, buoyed atop greasy ball bearings and a cushioned carpet. Dad sat, delegating all of himself to my guidance. One look, and my father, the phantom of endless energy in my childhood reemerged a younger man, a changed man. I smelled him, brushed my hands against the folds of his jacket.

The walker, Dad, and I stopped just at the apartment front door, where he reached for his house keys. I had them in my hand. I made sure he grasped them firmly before letting go. Because he couldn't see, he now depended on feeling.

"Thank you," he said. "I can make it on my own from here. That was such a nice dinner you served me tonight. Your sushi was so good, just how Mom used to make it."

Dad's eyes brightened for a moment, and I thought he actually noticed me this time, not blinded as he normally was. I stayed around for some moments while he puttered about his apartment putting things in order before going to bed. I wanted him safe before I left. Giving him a hug and after saying good night, I walked hand-in-hand with my seven-year-old daughter down the hall corridor and out to the car.

When we got home, I looked to the west, now completely dark after sunset, hoping to see something. The sky was black. The waxing moon had already dropped below the horizon.

CANNED PEACHES

A can of cling peaches opens with a swooshing sound of air rushing inward as the can opener bites into metal. The sweet aroma of cooked peaches escapes. I breathe in, inhale. A translucent, syrupy liquid submerges the severed lid, and I wind the can opener blade completely about the edges, then gingerly lift a sharp tin ridge with my fingers.

The yellow halves of peaches shine in this viscous syrup; my mouth waters as I dip in a spoon. Floating in the glossy medium, slick and wet, the peach evades my attempts to grab it, sliding this way and that. Spoon and rounded flesh skate next to each other. I manage to lift one peach half out of the can, dripping a line of syrup onto the counter and to my bowl. I try getting another. The second is easier and two peach halves meet, one sliding atop the other. Skinned, pitted, and cooked, this peach resembles little of its former self, scooped into the shape of a full moon. I bite. This peach tastes like candy.

This 9-ounce can holds eight halves, a total of four peaches. I paid $2.49 for it. That makes each whole peach worth about sixty cents. I can't help but calculate. I should know. Dad was never paid that much for his peaches, though. He was lucky to get a hundred dollars a ton for what he sent to the cannery. To think now that my father made a living and raised three daughters by farming cling peaches is amazing. I bite into the peach half, feel my teeth tear into flesh. It is chewy. That's the spirit of a cling. There's a wholesome body to the fruit that withstands the ordeal of harvest and its sometimes brutal transport to the cannery. So different is the cling compared to the freestone, the kind of peach sold fresh in the produce section of the grocery store, carefully picked and packed into separate slots on a small, plastic tray. The freestone is delicate. The pit separates easily from the flesh; and when this fruit is cooked, its texture withers in comparison to that of the cling, the king, in my opinion, of cooked peaches.

I imagine that few who taste this fruit hear the lyrical voices of the Mexican braceros as they had picked cling peaches, dropping them into their belly-covering canvas picking bags strapped onto their waists and shoulders and then dumping them into wooden bins. But I do, and as I suck on the juices of the peaches circling in my bowl, the songs and whistles of those farm workers crescendo.

I immerse my spoon into syrup, scoop it across the peach half and watch the juices run off the sides like water beading down the window in a rainstorm. Then I see my father through a distortion, though the developing haze of fog and mist, holding a clear plastic umbrella in the shape of a mushroom above him. He is in a forest green rain jacket and rain pants with a hood over his head. On his face he wears goggles and a carbon filter mask. I can't see much of him. I see only his green tent. He drives a tractor pulling a spray rig that's roaring as loud as a jet engine and sending a mist of chemicals arching into the tree rows. The peach leaves and branches batter and whip against each other in the artificial wind that gusts from the back of the spray rig. When finished, those things touched by the spray glisten with moisture.

I smell it, an acrid, sulfuric odor creeping inside the closed windows of our farmhouse; and I feel the vibration of the screeching propeller blades of the sprayer through my feet on the floor. I am here and my dad is out there, out in the thick of it. It's for the peaches, I know. It is his way of protecting them, and in a way, of protecting me.

I swallow another piece of cooked peach flesh, feel it slide down my throat. My father and the Mexicans braceros disappear. I am alone again, it's just me; and I welcome this peach, my old friend.

GETTING LUCKY

Yesterday it rained cats and dogs, the kind of precipitation driven in slanted sheets. Today, thin, wispy clouds roll past me in front of a gusty headwind, the last of a storm front piling against the Sierras to the east with fat, billowy cumulonimbus clouds hugging above mauve mountains.

A brisk gust whistles through the trees. It pushes me from behind as I jog. A viscous transparency tussles my ponytail, swats my face. I close my eyes and feel a pressure pursuing me. Between abrupt wind bursts, there are surprising periods of silence, when the wind forgets to blow or takes a breath. It is in these kinds of moments when I can sense as if something is reaching towards me through a narrow band of energy.

To the east lies Sacramento. I am thirty miles from my mother's birthplace, her childhood home. She might have experienced similar kinds of seasonal winds pushing and pulling from all directions. Could what have happened to her then resemble anything I was feeling now? I imagine her a slight teenager, a blossoming woman of seventeen, with wind blowing on her face, mussing her hair, pulling at her skirt and blouse. Might she have looked out west to where I was standing now and known that a daughter in her future would be running along that very same horizon?

It was just sixty-five years ago that my mother was evacuated from her home in Sacramento. Executive Order 9066, issued by President Franklin D. Roosevelt on February 19, 1942, ordered her and all other persons of one-sixteenth or more Japanese ancestry to leave the West Coast of the United States. It was an abrupt change, sending people packing, selling their belongings, abandoning cars, furniture, businesses, and their homes. In less than a week the wind had scoured the valley, knocked down my mother, her family and friends, and blown her first to a hastily constructed assembly center at a racetrack on the Fresno fairgrounds, and later east across the country to a camp in Jerome, Arkansas, a place of alligators, chiggers, and fireflies. It was there she adjusted to a new life. She lived in a barracks within barbed wire while the second war of the world raged forth in Europe and Asia.

Mom wouldn't talk with me about camp life. She skirted my questions and gave short answers. I learned that broaching the subject was taboo.

She would say, "Why, that was over fifty years ago. I can't remember." The corners of her mouth turned down, her lips puckered in a sour expression.

Her stilted mannerisms had a discomfiting effect on me, making me feel as if I was doing something wrong; I was crossing into forbidden territory. Her silence then puzzled me, but now I believe it had something to do with forgetting and forgiving. The silent, unspoken injustices never mentioned to us kids buffered me from ever having known there might have been a difference in being who I was, of Japanese descent, and that somehow I might have been considered a lesser person because of it. Mom didn't say what bad things had been done to her. She wanted that left behind. It has taken me awhile, and I still am not sure, but I think now I might better understand.

She had said that inside her barracks, ropes strung from wall to wall hung wool blankets for room dividers, the only sense of privacy family members could have in their living quarters. Children, parents, and grandparents had to adjust to tight living arrangements within a space for a few cots and minimal furnishings. Several families could reside in a single barracks. I can't recall hearing my mom complain about camp. She did, though, mention some things with a hint of enthusiasm. She had said moths chewed into the wool, peppering the blankets with holes. Even the wooden walls had gaping openings in them where knotholes had fallen out. Mom closed her thumb and forefinger together into a small circle, and then drew them towards one eye. She said,

"You could see lots of things through those holes." She giggled and spoke no more. I was left to imagine.

There had been a woman who used to stand throughout the day at the outside corner of the barracks, always in a black dress and carrying a black umbrella above her.

"She looked like Mary Poppins," my mother had said.

Then one morning the woman was not in her usual place; this time she was standing outside the barracks waist deep in water, in a big, rain barrel to be used for firefighting protection. Stoically unmoving, this Mary Poppins figure held open the black umbrella above her head.

Changing direction, I turn into the headwind. I find myself no longer floating. I am now fighting to move forward, the wind protesting, I am jogging into that which attempts to bolt me backwards. North wind blows not so friendly now. I lean forward, lift my knees and drive my way towards home.

My dad was drafted into the military in April 1941. While my mom was settling into life in the Japanese internment camp, my dad had already served a year in the United States Army. He trained in a town near Fort Lewis, Washington; in Kansas; and at Camp Savage, Minnesota. During the war, he was stationed in Brisbane, Australia; his last year was in the Philippines. Although my father never lived in an internment camp as my mother had, he did describe to me some instances of discrimination.

He had said that after Japan bombed Pearl Harbor on December 7, 1941, he and the other Japanese Americans in basic training in his unit were stripped of their rifles. Dad complained that he was no longer allowed to participate in military maneuvers, that he wasn't considered trustworthy. He was assigned to cleaning the camp and the latrines. "Menial work," he called it. It was then that my father decided to become a camp cook, because he knew at least he'd be guaranteed of getting fed, and for him, being able to eat had always been important. And eat well as a cook he did, because eventually my dad worked up to the rank of staff sergeant, and he and the other cooks who he supervised saved the best portions of meat, the filet mignon, for themselves.

While on leave at the port of Oakland before departing overseas, my father and his fellow Japanese-American servicemen were restricted on base, the fallout of Executive Order 9066 prohibiting them from leaving the confines of the military zone. By that time, all other Japanese Americans on the West Coast had been evacuated to assembly centers or internment camps elsewhere. Dad said his commanding officer had felt sorry for his men. He told them to go to a bar, have a good time, and, if anyone questioned, say they were Chinese.

"You see, all the Chinese running around San Francisco and Oakland back then wore these big buttons on their shirts that said 'I Am Chinese.' Our commander got some buttons for us to wear that day, and nobody bothered us."

On a military ship, my dad departed from Oakland to Brisbane. He liked the swells, the unpredictability of motion. While others were seasick, my father was craving more action.

"The bigger the waves, the better I liked them," he had said to me. I can imagine my dad grinning at the bow of that ship, getting sprayed and sloshed with salt water, his stance akimbo as the world around him rocked in fury.

BRENDA NAKAMOTO

In Australia, at a Military Intelligence Service camp where prisoners of war were kept, Dad interacted with a captured Japanese naval officer. Dad wasn't sure of his exact rank, but he surmised this man was a very important person in Japan. Dad mentioned that the guys said he should be the one to take the officer his food, him being Japanese and all, and Dad agreed and prepared his meal along with nigiri that he made special for him. When he entered the man's quarters, an army tent surrounded by fence, Dad bowed courteously, presented the food, and said, *arigatoo*, thank you.

"Why say arigatoo?" I asked.

"It seemed like the appropriate thing to do. I didn't know much Japanese and it was the only word that came to mind at the time."

After listening to my father, I thought about how there might be a kind of respect between people, even between those from opposite political positions and social ranks, like my father, this lowly cook, and the high-ranking official from the country of our enemy.

Dad added that there had been an interpreter in his unit whose brother served in the Japanese Imperial Army and who had been captured and was now a prisoner of war. The interpreter had been raised in America while his brother was raised in Japan. It was not uncommon for some Japanese families to be split in that way. Dad's friend the interpreter requested leave time and was reported to have visited his imprisoned brother.

Dad could have signed up for another term of service with the army at the end of his fourth year. He had been asked to continue; and he could have been promoted. But he declined. He decided to go home, to go back to the farm waiting for him in Gridley. And back home in the valley is where he met my mother and eventually married. Even though she and her family had moved to Arkansas during the camp years, after the war was over, her father had called his dispersed children across the U.S. back home to the California valley, because it was time to return.

"You never can tell what's going to happen," my dad said to me. "Sometimes you get lucky."

His words rumble in my head. With each step towards home, I hear his voice. The past is gone, and whatever has happened before exists only in memory. One never knows what lies ahead. The north wind gusts, and I think I must live for today, for each moment. Persistence—that's what my parents and grandparents had. If I can overcome now but a fraction of what they had faced, I will be truly lucky.

BRENDA NAKAMOTO

PEACH COBBLER

Today, I am making peach cobbler. The May weather hasn't decided whether to warm or cool, and this indecision jogs my senses—hot, then cold; rain, then fog; blossoms, then fruit. These juxtapositions can be reason to celebrate; I experience both ends of a spectrum almost simultaneously. Spring weather roars like a lion one day with thunderstorms and gusty winds; it purrs the next with the buzzing of bees and warm sunshine. Let us applaud this season with a cheer—come get fresh-baked peaches swirled within a crispy crust: good old-fashioned peach cobbler. Mmm.

I start with flour for the crust. My daughter stands on a step-stool and holds a sifter while I pour in the measured flour.

"Where does flour come from?" she asks.

I hesitate. She doesn't know where flour comes from? My daughter? This mother grew up on a peach farm next to a field of over a hundred acres of wheat. Walking the perimeter, I'd watch wheat sprout from tender green shoots and stretch to tall, amber spikes with heavy heads. I'd follow dust devils higher than the valley oaks twisting over that open field.

"Flour comes from a wheat berry, and flour is the wheat grain ground to a fine powder," I answer.

"What kind of berry? Like grapes?" she asks. Her large, brown eyes don't quite understand.

I never realized before how quickly a simple subject can transform into a bear of an answer. Obviously, I forget she knows little of my past, of my history that so clearly defines the answer. How can I communicate to eight-year-old eyes?

"Like rice, wheat berries are the seeds of wheat that grow at the tip of the plant, and when fully developed, the heads of seeds are cut and separated from the non-edible part, the chaff."

"Oh," she answers, the glow in her eyes falters; I think I am losing her. Make it easy for her, make it real. I should show her a stalk of wheat. It should be simple. Walk out the back door, go fifty yards past the drain ditch and pick one. In my mind I start to go outside, but I'm not there anymore, not back on that farm next to the wheat field, the peach orchards, the walnut trees and pears.

It is difficult to not think otherwise, having been saturated in the farm life my entire childhood. Back then, I was growing up with agriculture. I breathed it every day, from the sunrise of spring blossoms to the sunsets of fruity harvests. Almost everyone I knew had some connection to the job of raising food. So this nagging thought—my daughter doesn't even know where flour comes from—bothers me.

Noriko sifts. Being more involved with the baking process than getting her question answered, she quickly forgets, infatuated with this gadget with rotating blades that pushes flour, sugar, and salt back and forth through a screen. It grates and rasps when she squeezes the handle. She giggles. This is a new toy. The weight of powdery flour softens the biting sound of metal blade against mesh, bleating like the background tone of fingers drumming lightly against the surface of wood; and the mixed, dry ingredients soon pile under the sifter into a little mountain in the bowl with each squeeze and release of the handle. How the mound puffs up like freshly laid white snow on a peak. I think of Coast Range mountains to the west, with their striated golden ridges folding through foothills. I think of the solitary peaks of the valley's lone Sutter Buttes, the smallest mountain range in the world, sometimes dusted in snow in cold winters. These eroded peaks, the remnants of a once-active volcano in the Central Valley, glow purple-green in the winter mornings and burnt-orange in the summer sunsets. I could see them outside the farmhouse back door, always there—south-southwest. I think of home, that place that never moved, a square white stucco house next to hundreds of peach trees and a county road, five miles from the nearest city. It would always be there for me, and in some ways, it still is.

Wheat plants sprout from seeds. Peach trees sprout from seeds. Yet Dad never sowed peach seeds in his orchard. If he did that, the time from initial planting to viable harvest would lengthen greatly. As it was, it took several years for him to get a sizeable crop out of new trees planted from bare roots. Timing was everything, diversification a must. Dad had replaced some old, sick almond trees in the orchard with saplings from the local nursery. They were grafted, having a different rootstock than the rest of the tree. But something peculiar happened. Dad waited several years for the trees to bear nuts, yet there weren't any, only short, stocky shrubs with lots of foliage. They would have made excellent hedges. He pulled them out of the ground and started over.

"Mommy, can't you hurry?" Noriko's impatient voice jars my thoughts. She wipes a hand on her face, pushing back a lock of auburn hair from her forehead and leaving a smudge of flour on her cheek. She smiles. She looks so unlike me. I see some of her father's traits in her, the genes of his dishwater blond hair and blue eyes underlying her Asian features. I can't help but smile, because I know despite my comparisons she is herself—not half me, not half him. She is Noriko.

I scrape shortening into a measuring cup, pressing down the fat, releasing the trapped air. I tap the spatula on the cup and finish off with a leveling stroke across the top. Noriko stands in front of the mixing bowl, making me stretch my arms to the side. It doesn't matter that I can't see what I am doing, because in no time she's going to be the one making a peach cobbler all on her own. I figure she should now be the one to get a ringside seat.

I add the shortening to the dry ingredients. The white, oily blob falls smack in the middle of the floury mountain. Proper pie crust needs fat to keep it light and flaky. I show my daughter how to use the pastry blender to cut into the shortening. I slice into the fat, the half-dozen wire dividers of the utensil soon making thin strips of the shortening. Noriko takes over.

"This is fun," she gloats. With ambitious, subsequent chops, she works the pastry blender, smoothing the lines of distinction between shortening and flour until eventually everything in the bowl shrinks to the size of rice kernels. That's right. This is how good pie crust is made: flour dry and puffy, shortening rich and greasy. It is this commixing of unlike substances that is so wonderful. Flour without fat would bake dense and hard as a brick. Fat without flour would bake to a sloppy, greasy puddle. Noriko scrapes the bowl one last time with the pastry blender, tapping metal against ceramic. I think the sounds of cooking are just as pleasurable as the smelling and the tasting.

Snip, clip, clip. The percussion of pruning shears cuts through the air. In the middle of winter, Dad clipped branches off the peach trees. He worked with artistic precision, trimming hangers off the lower limbs that splayed off the main trunk, and he cropped the topmost branches in a sharp crew cut. The majority of the fruit would set in the upper canopy. Space needed to be left below to allow for machinery to move underneath. He pruned, keeping those summer peaches in mind, and he saved some of the low suckers for producing fruit with the next season. Early on, Dad used ten- or twelve-foot wooden ladders to prune. Up and down, up and down, tree after hundredth tree, in the frosty, cold air against the backdrop of crisp blue December sky, Dad and Uncle Bob manicured the leafless branches. Pruning was done when the trees were dormant, when they were asleep for the winter and the sap was not running. Pruning in summer would be like inviting all their blood to flow out.

Later, Dad experimented with stilts. They were eight-foot high rods of aluminum, similar to the kind used in parades with a person walking high above the crowd dressed as Uncle Sam. Same idea. When Dad strapped the stilts to his work boots and stood up, he became Meccano Man with legs of steel, taller than any human, and he didn't need a ladder to get him to the top tree branches. Snip, clip, clip. Mom wanted me to find Dad, tell him it's time for lunch. I step outside the back door, stop and listen. I am looking for RoboFarmer. I can find him just by listening for the crackling sound of the transistor radio he keeps rubber-banded to his belt. If I hear an agitated, high-pitched voice of the radio talk show host like Ira Blue wafting through the air, I know I've found him.

The crust recipe asks for one egg and $\frac{1}{4}$ cup of water. I whip them together and work this into the flour mixture until a ball forms; the dough sticks with a glutinous adhesion and has a good intuitive feel to it—not too wet or too dry. Then I refrigerate it. I can address the peach filling now. Without the filling, the crust is nothing. They both need each other. In another bowl, I place a cup of sugar, ground nutmeg and cinnamon. Spices help bring out the essence of a dish; they add flavor and richness to the peaches that alone the fruit would not have. So plain looks a cup of white sugar heaped into a bowl. I smell the nutmeg and cinnamon, but I cannot smell the sugar. In this state, it might be too far removed from its history. We've done all this preparatory work and haven't even touched the peaches. Dad sold the farm over a decade ago and we don't have our own fresh homegrown fruit anymore. I bought some peaches from the grocery store, probably raised in southern California, where the weather is hotter and the crops have ripened sooner. Grasping a peach in my hand, I cannot help but consider it second rate. After all, Dad was awarded a prize one year for raising the best-quality cling peaches in his area. His picture decorated a page in the Gridley *Herald*. With a peeler, I start at the stem of the peach and circle around the fruit, separating pink and yellow skin from the orange flesh underneath. A long strand of peel hangs below my hands and drops to the sink below. In this naked state, the peach loses its identity. I may not have a farm anymore, but I still have memory.

Spring bursts into the valley with a gush of color. Having seen only fog and rain and overcast skies for the past months, I anxiously await the first swelling of buds on the bare tree branches. Then an explosion of blossoms from the almonds snowballs simultaneously across the orchard. With petals of white and stamens of yellow, the burst of color jolts my senses, and I am awakened in this balmy season. The crows like it too, and in late afternoons, hundreds of the glossy-feathered birds gather together, and the cacophony of their cackling can be heard from half a mile away. Not long afterwards, the peach trees push open their buds, and after enjoying the almonds, now I inhale the scent from peach tree blossoms.

Noriko combines the peach slices with sugar and cinnamon, melting them into a syrupy coating with each flip of the wooden spatula. Unable to contain herself, she grabs a spoon from the drawer and dips it into the bowl. That's the best part of baking. It's sampling part of the raw ingredients before baking. It's the tentative dipping of a finger into the batter before disappearing in one's lips.

"It tastes good, Mommy," she says, licking another spoonful of syrup with her tongue.

"And you helped make it," I compliment her. I hug my little girl, my little one who has to stand on the stepstool, the one who laughs and smiles for almost no reason at all. Her round cheeks plump to a rosy red. Her dimples dent small hollows near her eyes. How my mother would have enjoyed meeting my daughter, the granddaughter she never knew, this happy girl bursting with so much joy.

Mom and Auntie Sumi and cousins Diane and Lucy pick lug boxes of peaches from our orchard, our voices filled with laughter as we maneuver the old jalopy from tree to tree. Mom and her sister chatter like chickens and they banter back and forth, sounding so much alike that I think I have

BRENDA NAKAMOTO

two moms. No, actually, it is so loud that I've gained a whole crowd of moms. We pick our fill, then park the jalopy under the thick branches of the big walnut tree that shade our house and Mom's prized dichondra lawn. Now the work gets tedious. One by one, Mom and Auntie Sumi peel each peach. Then, with a pitter, they jab the blade inside, twist and turn and in one fluid motion separate the stone from the fruit. Finally, they halve each peach and toss the finished product into a clean wooden lug box. I watch. I can't peel, nor can I pit. But their hands move smoothly and swiftly, and they talk and giggle as they spend hours in the shade. Morning light drifts into long afternoon shadows and I wait and wonder how much aphid sap has drifted down on me. One thing I have learned for sure: Never leave anything under a walnut tree; it will be sticky the next morning.

Nearing the end of rolling pie crust, Noriko and I say to heck with weaving the dough and lazily crisscross what flattened crust is left and drape it over the pie tin full of peach slices, sugar, and spice. That's cheating. I know I will never be as good a cook as my mother, nor will I be as good a farmer as my father. I could probably not outlast the stamina of my grandparents, who spent hours every day in the fields. Some things are just not meant to be. But how lucky I am to be here now, standing in the shadow of those who have passed before. Because of them, I am making peach cobbler with my daughter. Perhaps parts of their voices are speaking through me.

The timer rings and the cobblers are done. I pull them from the oven. They smell yummy and are drippy and syrupy with the scent of spring gushing through my kitchen. Noriko's face lights up, and she oohs and ahhs and claps her hands. "I didn't know that peaches could be this wonderful!" she exclaims. I hug her. I am proud of my little girl. Our crusts wouldn't win any accolades, but the essence of peach cobbler is still there, even though it is not blue-ribbon quality. And the essence, I believe, must be the most important thing.

HANDS

Hands, fat and wide like old tree stumps, cracked and wrinkled and engraved dark brown. Fingers stubby and wide, worked daily by grasping, clutching, and throwing. Palms with bumps of coarse white skin, the pads indented and scared. Calloused and thick, these are farmer's hands, my daddy's hands, and those of his peach orchard neighbors. These fingers wind the socket wrench swinging in pendulum motion, the whinnies and squeaks of a handle rotated back and forth. These hands covered in oil, stained in a patina of spider webbing, etched on human skin. These hands are immersed in turpentine, splashed and rubbed. Pumice soap scours in between the lines, where Daddy wrings his hands, bent over the cement laundry tub. Below dribbles murky water draining from underneath the faucet. These hands embedded in dirt smelling of tractor grease and starting fluid and paint remover. Hands grasp onto peaches or walnuts or kiwis, and what you notice first might not be the fruit, but the chunky paws of those farmer hands that are made by pulling branches and pushing off the limbs from the first cut of a chainsaw. A hand jerks the steering wheel on a tractor pulling a great harrow that with gleaming silver disks churns and rakes the field. Those stubby thumbs of the tractor driver open and close against those just-as-stout forefingers, and fingers together clutch and relax, day in and day out. These fingers and hands mature. They work together. They are a force to be reckoned with, tumbling a four-foot square wooden picking bin from the top of a high stack to the ground. These farming hands one can only earn, one doesn't take shortcuts to get these hands. They wave a quick morning hello at sunrise, accompanied by a sharp whistle blown from two fingers inserted into lips. A hand waves goodbye in the settling dust of twilight, the truck lights dimming after the moan of the engine fades away.

Harold Nakamoto as an army cook

BRENDA NAKAMOTO

LISTENING TO UNLUCKY LUCK

Daddy prays for me.

"At night I ask God to watch over you and Shawn and the kids. I tell him about the people at Covell Gardens. I ask God to help you rent your house."

I hold an old picture of Dad in my hands, amber and golden and faded from the clearer black and white it must have been long ago. His hands are on a box, and there's another box on the ground marked with the upside-down word "vinegar." He's pulling it down a short wooden ramp at his feet. Dad grins from behind a white knee-length apron on top of his military uniform and he dons a crisp cap.

He says, "I was in the Philippines the last year before I was discharged. My squad leader offered me a promotion if I reenlisted and I thought about it, but said no because I had asked Baachan, and she wanted me to come back home. I was sorry afterwards. Boy, was I sorry!"

Well, yes, he was sorry because the hard life started all over for him, having to be a farm laborer after having had three square meals a day cooking as a mess hall sergeant for the previous four years. For dad, military life had been a good one. But it was a time of new choices and decisions. Ojiisan had died from tuberculosis during the Japanese internment, and now Baachan wanted Dad to take care of her.

Dad laughs and smiles with a sheepish grin, and I know he wants to talk, to tell me his regrets, to add more misery to all the bum luck he thinks he's had this unlucky life. Mom isn't here to listen to him. Sometimes I think he waits the entire week for me to visit, just so that he can tell me things. He might even invent tasks for me to do to see him more often: "Brenda, can you bring me a bag of hard candy, coffee flavored, anything? I need it right away."

He says, "Up until fourth grade, I had a good life and I was happy. Then my father became a farm laborer and we moved to Oroville and lived in trucks and tents. Baachan was a purdy woman, but when I was in the eighth grade, she got burned and then she didn't look so good."

I remember that story about the fire that badly burned my baachan, disfiguring the skin on her arms and legs when she rescued Uncle Ray from their burning home.

Uncle Ray used to toss me high in the air and bounce me on top of his shoulders where I could reach up and almost touch the ceiling. So warm up there, riding Uncle Ray like he's my horsey on that winter evening with the gas furnace turned up toasty. He'd visit us at our house and give me presents like a tiny toy sewing machine whose needle cut paper as I wove in and out of the sheets. He started me on my career in sewing, my streak of winning blue and red ribbons at the county fairs and 4-H dress reviews. Uncle Ray wrote letters to Baachan, one of which I still have stored in the attic. "Dearest Mom" it began, ending with "Your always loving son, Ray."

Baachan saved him; she had carried him to me.

"Baachan was a smart woman," my dad says.

Uncle Ray disappears out of communication from our family for a long period of time. We don't know why exactly; even Dad when I ask him never understood why Ray didn't call or visit us anymore. Maybe it was because my dad and mom tried to set him up with a lady friend and it failed, and Uncle Ray might have felt he had lost face. Many decades later, he and Dad and Uncle Bob reunite. It was almost like nothing had ever happened.

"I was my father's own bad luck," Dad volunteers.

Daddy tells me that when he and Uncle Bob were kids, they

played with matches and burned down the barn with some of the belongings of Ojiisan's brother who had returned to Japan. The fire jumped to the Caucasian neighbor's property and burned up his garage and a Model T. Ojiisan came home and chased the boys with a stick. Before the fire, Dad remembers plenty of food, nice clothes, and good times. After the fire, another fire mysteriously razed the restaurant that Baachan and Ojiisan ran in Yuba City, ending their culinary careers. That's when food started getting scarce. Dad doesn't know how the debt was repaid, if ever.

Manila 1945

"After the occupation of the Philippines by the Japanese, I was worried how the people were going to treat me. But, you know, they were pretty nice. Children came to our barracks with one-gallon cans and we'd dump in food for them to take home to eat with their families."

"I used to drive the mess hall truck or the munitions truck and take things like flour and staples into the city and dump it on the streets. We'd agree beforehand on a place."

I'd heard that one before, the little bit of black-market side business my dad had run, the one he now regrets and that weighs on his conscience. "I could have been thrown into the brig," he says.

"God is punishing me now for all the bad things I have done."

I listen and see through his eyes now—like the time he helped me prune my backyard peach tree while he sat in his walker and he couldn't see, but he could instruct by hearing the buzz of my handsaw cutting into the wood and the crack of the tree limb as it fell. He was alarmed I was pruning too much! There's a smell of sunshine on skin and sweat. Dad opens up a whole new world for me, one begging to be rediscovered: scarred and blemished, loved and cherished.

BRENDA NAKAMOTO

HOLDING ONTO SIGHT

sometime in 2005

"What time is it?" Dad asks, after calling me one night on the telephone. In the last year, I've watched his eyesight spiral downward. He recently lost most of his remaining vision with the advancement of glaucoma, a disease he's lived with for decades and that has gradually blinded him by damaging his optic nerves, making them unable to send transmissions to the brain.

"It's 10 PM," I shout. He's hard of hearing, too. At eighty-seven years old, he's got only one good ear left and even that barely functions.

"What?" he asks.

"10 PM, night time. It's after dinner," I say. I repeat my answer in as many ways that I can creatively muster, figuring one of those he can understand. I enunciate slowly.

"Oh?" he says and then adds, "I just got dressed for breakfast. Oh golly."

I can't help but laugh and think how funny this is: Ten o'clock at night, and my father thinks it's breakfast. Then again, another part of me feels this is quite pitiful, I can't see a bit of humor in it at all. Everything for him now is dark, only shadows of faces, the outlines of the body. Light is gray, gray is black. My poor father can't see.

So this is how everlasting night is. He lives in the evening, when the sun doesn't shine and all is twilight.

Sleep. He sleeps after breakfast, after lunch, and after dinner. His diurnal clock can't function. The brain tells him he is in shadow where no light falls.

I watch my dad float his hands on the bathroom counter, find his dentures, finger where the groove of the ridge is, pull out the denture adhesive tube and lay a line of cream on top of the edges. He works with a system, a method of logical progression, marking medicine bottles with rubber bands, putting papers in big envelopes, putting other types of papers in little envelopes, big words scrawled on paper notes taped to the wall, paper clips in sections of his pocket calendar, paper clips rubber-banded to the medicine bottles, every medicine container placed within its own section in a cardboard box he taped together from empty cereal boxes, eyeglasses laid on top of his night stand, pens and pencils always in a cup next to the telephone. He fumbles, walking with a hand along the wall, and hobbles to the chair where his pants are hung over the back exactly where he put them the night before, with the belt already in place, a small, zippered leather pouch with his eye medications hung between the loops. For him even in darkness, the sun will still rise; it will soon be morning. He knows that. He has his chores to do.

Some systems fail, though, like the talking wristwatch. He couldn't hear it. But if he ever gets off track, can't tell what's going up or coming down, he'll call, usually at an unusually early hour in the morning, especially on Saturdays. One of us will answer. This time it is my husband speaking in a groggy voice; and my dad is on the other end of the line.

"Shawn, what time and what day is it?"

Mother's Day 2008

Those eyes gaze at shadows, the pupils large and round like dilated owl eyes. The right one is glazed over from exposure because the eyelid won't completely close, the cornea dry and opaque, its clarity smeared under the goo of lubricating eye-drops. The left one, not much better, follows the sound of my voice. Dad turns his face towards me, the cracked, white foam of dry spittle creasing the edges of his lips. I tap him on the shoulder and ask him if he wants to eat. He always wants to eat, to go to a restaurant, that's one of his favorite things to do. He can't turn me down; but today he does. The staff is worried. He's not eating, hardly walking, and I'm told he's hallucinating. He's dreaming he's back on the farm, calling out that he's working on a tractor, and he's very convincing. That's not so bad, I think, to believe you're back on the farm. I listen to him, notice his labored breathing interspersed with squeaky wheezes, coarse and drawn. How it rattles and rasps at times, as if air squeezed through a tiny opening of a balloon.

I don't realize how weak he is until I try to get him into the car, our sport utility vehicle. Dad has commented how he liked our car that reminded him of a truck, where he could grab the handle next to the sun visor and rest a palm on the door and then hop onto the passenger seat.

Today he hasn't the strength. He labors, he moans. I coax him, "Bring up your left leg. Lift it. Come on, there."

"I can't do it," he says finally after much fidgeting.

I know he means it. I am about ready to go home and drive back the small sedan that's lower to the ground. Time is rushing me, though. We'll be late for his doctor's appointment.

"Heidi," I call out to my dad's caregiver beside me. "We'll lift him. Let's try."

Heidi grabs his legs and I wrap my arms around his chest.

"Oh, oh, oh, oh," he yells as we two women try to manhandle all 135 pounds of him.

He's limp and leans off kilter. I think moving a sack of potatoes would have been easier. His body is that of a Gumby doll, appendages soft and bendy. A few inches of his buttocks we manage to get onto the edge of the seat, and then we push back his hips, scoot his legs forward and underneath the dash. We did it. He leans sideways in the seat; I pull him upright, snap the seatbelt over him, moving him like a sack, moving him like a sack....

He's really more like a sack of prunes, the fresh, French plum type, just like we used to farm in Gridley, back in the old days when prunes were called prunes, not plums, whether fresh or dried. His shirt and jacket that I feel against my chest are really a heavy woven, burlap tarp that's bundled in prunes and itches my skin and smells not only like oily, dusty twine, but it's imbued with this sweetness, a really sweet sweetness. If you've ever driven by a Sunsweet prune dehydrating plant, you will know what I mean. Fresh prunes have this fragrance that's rich and creamy in texture like canned milk.

You see, the shaker tractor has just finished shaking the prune tree and is now detaching its crab-like claw from the base of a trunk; and the two large sections of burlap spread underneath the branches like a wide picnic blanket are now entirely covered in a thick layer of purple fruit and leaves. The tractor rattles and jars the summer silence and put-put-puts its way to the next tree, ready to clutch its greased black, rubber block pads around the next victim.

Daddy and Uncle Bob and a couple of our Mexican workmen are pounding the branches of that tree with football-sized rubber mallets on the end of long wooden handles and belting the last of the fruit off the limbs. Then they are together, grabbing the corners of the burlap tarps and dragging them hammock style to the four-foot square wooden bin, where— with a few synchronized swings and yells of the ol' heave ho—the bulk of the burlap sheet and the bundled prunes are boosted and shoved into the bin. Once inside, the burlap is pulled out like it's a scarf emerging from a magician's hat. Then the other burlap, lying under the other half of the prune tree, is dragged to the bin and Daddy is there manhandling it all by himself. I might even run to him to help and I'll push on that big old gunny sack, dropping those plump prunes the size of chubby thumbs inside the bin. You can hear those little babies plopping against the slats.

My main job, though, is a prune picker, and Mom and Auntie Chi and Rod and Glen and I are on the soft, plowed ground on our hands and knees with our buckets between our legs or in front of us, and we're picking up the extra prunes that were flung far onto the dirt or somehow squeezed in the grass between the trunk and the burlap. Auntie Chi is like a juggler, and those prunes are flying out of her hands and rainbowing into her five-gallon steel bucket. I don't know how she can be so fast and agile. For Rod, Glen, and me with our gallon-sized plastic buckets, it's more like an Easter egg hunt, and we'll whoop and holler if we find a plateful-sized pile of prunes in the crotch of the tree or in the grass because then it's easy pickings and we are competing with each other to see who can pick the most buckets, because we're getting paid five cents a bucket; and it's our goal each day to make a hundred.

Vitals. Take the vital signs, the doctor says to the nurse after looking at my father. Dad is sleeping in the wheel chair, head slanted down at an angle. The nurse comments that she can't register a reading on one of the instruments that's connected by a long cord to his finger. It measures oxygen level. Together they work the monitoring box and after some moments, the doctor says his oxygen level is low, it's ninety-two, and she listens to his chest and hears something coming from his lungs. I don't know exactly what ninety-two means, but I accept that it likely means something not good. Within fifteen minutes after bypassing emergency from the Urgent Care office, I am wheeling Dad into the hospital.

Again, I am working with someone, and this time it is a nurse and together we are guiding Dad from the wheelchair and into the bed. I am on one side, the nurse is on the other. Dad shuffles warily in short, trepid steps. Come forward. Come forward. That's right. Oh, he's so cute, she says. He really follows instructions well.

Wait a minute; I don't think you really know my father.

In bed, he leans on a pillow and I see and hear him give a sigh. Again, he starts to fall asleep. Vitals, vital signs, I hear these words bounced in the room. Phlebotomist. Just a pinch, you'll feel a pinch. I'm glad I'm not there in bed getting my blood drawn. I'm asked to leave the room as the x-ray machine is wheeled in and I sit on a chair in the hallway and start jotting notes. It gives me something to do, to record my thoughts, makes me look like I'm doing something purposeful when really I'm feeling as helpless and alien in this hospital setting as a wallflower at a dance. I glance into Dad's room and see him surrounded by three women: one trying to draw blood, another waiting to get him positioned for the x-rays, another doing I don't know what she's doing. Three women, especially one who says that he's cute. That can't be so bad.

I wonder why Dad is always surrounded by women. He had three daughters and a wife. He has a staff of women at his home care. He's now got all these women sweet-talking with him and I hear him chuckle faintly. Life is good.

I stay with him a few hours, hours that are filled with commotion: tubes and needles going in, samples going out. Monitor, monitor, monitor. My, this hospital is a busy place. I tell him I have to go; I don't want to go. It's Mother's Day, and I'm being treated to a family outing to see an Alicia Keyes concert in Sacramento. I feel guilty leaving; I should be staying with him instead. But the pricey tickets were already purchased and if I don't go, then the kids and Shawn wouldn't go and I can't spoil the fun.

That night I don't know what I'm feeling. It's all so confusing, time revolving, singers singing, dancers dancing. All the glitter and glamour of Hollywood, this bombardment of rhythm and blues. Don't want to be here, really want to be here. Dad is

BRENDA NAKAMOTO

in the hospital again, he will get out of the hospital again or maybe this time he won't get out again. Who knows?

Jordin Sparks makes a guest appearance with Chris Brown, singing "No Air." I am moved, transformed, their lyrics buzzing through my head, snippets repeating—

no air

"Everybody, turn on your cell phones and wave your arms," Alicia tells us.

The lights go out in the entire arena, and we are shrouded in darkness with the exception of three tiers of luminous blue-green lights from cell phones swaying in rhythm to the music. I look up; I see around me this multi-layered sea of light—eerie, luminous, floating. My breath butterflies away. All of us strangers coming together in synchrony, Alicia and her backup singers chorus in the background. Maybe there is hope, not sure for what or for whom. Just hope that somehow there's sense in all this.

I can't breathe, not without air. But this song is winding through my head. I just can't get it out of my head, in and out, in my sleep, in my dreams, when I wake, when I ride my bike to work, when I walk down that hospital hallway....

"Intriguing, looking down into the water tank, down through the spout, into spooky darkness."

Yes, there was Daddy's water tank that he welded—well, not all of it. I think he got the basic ten-foot round cylinder from some farm equipment salesman or wherever farmers get their specialized kinds of gadgets. The water tank on wheels towed behind a tractor for watering down the dusty roads—that was all Daddy's idea. It was a big round metal tub sidelong on wheels, shaped like a gigantic bullet, a miniature gasoline tank, with a two-foot round opening on top, a circular snug fitting iron cap connected to the tank with chain, and welded handles on it so it could be easily pulled on and off. He painted it blood red, which lasted only a year or two before it faded to a dusty red-orange from weathering. Behind the tank a few feet off the ground is a linear contraption of four-inch round plumbing pipe, an enormous, long spaghetti noodle, just wide enough to cover the tire tracks as the tank was pulled forward. Dad drilled small holes into the metal pipe and he fashioned an on-and-off switch that regulated water gushing through the insides. One big jerk on the wire connected to the piping with my hands one way—a quick holler to my dad and then a leap onto the tractor seat next to him—and I was with him on a mission, speeding down the dusty orchard road, spreading a 10-foot-wide swath of showering water spraying from the back of the tank. He'd pull on the lever next to the steering wheel that throttled the gas—with a thrumming humming expelling from the tractor engine—and it was a bouncy, wind-in-the-face ride down that summer road between the peach and almond trees, with a sky starting to darken in that late afternoon light.

When we ran out of water, I'd clamber onto the top of that water tank and look into the chamber, empty. It was completely dark, even in that broad daylight of summer. It's the kind of tank that you holler into, and your echo is so immediate and intense you hear yourself as an opera star. Sound bounces back to you in stereo from the bowels of that tank. Mysterious, like there's some duplicate of myself down there that you can't see. Tra la la! Tra la la la la! Sing! We are so beautiful! Couldn't see through the darkness to the corners, though, not that a cylinder has any corners, just edges and a two-foot hole at the top. I'm precariously straddling that tank, the round sides of it underneath my thighs like I'm riding a horse, except I'm more than ten feet high and Daddy's pulling the water tank with a tractor up ahead, positioning it next to the irrigation water pump where he's rigged an even more elaborate plumbing system that diverts the water from moving horizontally across the orchard floor to vertically. It juts in 90-degree angles a few times until the pipe arches way up high above our heads and over the orchard road like a gigantic spigot, a cloth strapped around it to minimize splashing.

I jump off the tractor, flip the switch on the irrigation pump, hear the electric motor turning on. Then white water froths down the cement chute and onto the ground of the nearby peach trees. Flip up a lever on the side of the control panel and the vacuum and gurgling sound of water rushing up pipes overhead precedes a flush of water gushing out the spigot and down into the awaiting water tank. Dad, on the tractor, grins. He's trained me well. I cup my ears with my hands, the sound is so noisy.

Red-painted water tank leaves parts of itself on me, on my shirt smudged red, as I slide down its side, belly button forward, my knees red and dirty, my hands and feet muddy.

Looking into the water-filled tank, loaded to the brim, all glossy, blurry, mirror-like and refracting, I wonder, couldn't I just dive in? It's so dreadfully hot in summer. The chilled metal sides of the tank against my cheek and stomach are so refreshing. Feel that coolness under my face and stomach when I lie face down on that tank, clear, blue sky above, and shimmery liquid underneath. That round hole is black as midnight, but below, inside, I know that inviting water is there waiting. I just can't see it. Might I dive into the tank, swim like a goldfish in a black bowl, hold my breath, pull myself deep, and touch bottom?

no air

"Wanna do it?" I remember asking Rodney as we're eying that intriguing water in the water tank.

I know we wanted to, we most dreadfully wanted to. But we never did. Sometimes I think I saw myself submerged in that tank, my face upwards facing the sunlit round hole. It is so comforting in that icy, cold ground water in the just-filled tank, blackness around me. It's like someone had carved out an ice-fishing hole, and looking closer, there's Rodney peering down at me; I can see him smiling. That hole is white and clear, and bright sky is above. If I pop my head through the opening, I can raise my arms and just squeeze my shoulders through the edges to squiggle out of the tank and raise myself out. But nobody ever goes in, as inviting an idea as it seemed, for sometimes I thought I saw my own face looking at me when I looked at the water brimming to the edge of the hole, and I couldn't get out, like I was seeing through time or something, kind of like I'm seeing things right now.

After the concert, my ears are still burning when I lie down in bed. Even though it's after midnight, I have to wind down, drain away the excitement, try and exhale all those belted verses. Dad would have enjoyed the concert. He would have been able to feel the music through the sound waves pulsing against his body. He might have imagined what the dancers looked like. Maybe he could have seen the sparkle of Alicia Keyes's sequined white blouse glint off the spotlights. I wonder if he is doing okay.

I walk into his hospital room. The first thing Dad mumbles is that he's working underneath the truck and needs to buy some parts. That one flies by me and I nod and smile even though I know he can't see me. Then he asks me if I've eaten dinner. I answer that I've already eaten, I tell him that it's nine o'clock at night.

"Is that so?" he answers. He puts his attention on his blanket, fingering it with his hands. "Do you have a fork?"

"What for?" I ask.

"Well, I can't seem to get this to my mouth."

"That's your blanket, Dad, it's not food."

He gets this discouraged look on his face, with a squinting of his eyes and a tilt of his head, like he doesn't believe me.

"Who's sitting in that chair?"

"Nobody, Dad. That's my computer bag."

When I tell him that I have to go and we are saying goodbyes, he calls out and asks me, "Brenda, do you think you could drop by and pick me up an *Appeal-Democrat*? I mean, oh never mind." The *Appeal-Democrat* is a newspaper in Yuba City.

As I'm leaving, the nurse tells me he had been trying to get out of bed all afternoon, arguing that he had to grab a rope on the floor.

"Oh, he was a farmer. A farmer needs rope," I say, "He used to raise peaches."

The nurse adds, "He was pretty set he had to get it. He's strong, we had to struggle with him." She assures me he's doing well, the antibiotics are working, controlling the pneumonia.

"Yeah, that's my dad, strong-willed," I tell her. I laugh, at the same time, feel the back of my throat tighten. I thank her for all the things that she and everyone else at the hospital are doing for him and for me. I can't give him the kind of assistance he's receiving here. I walk down the hall. I am leaving because I have to escape. I'm on the downhill verge of feeling—I don't know what I'm feeling—this tightness in my chest. It's this going away thing that always gets to me.

No air, no air

We used to call them "steelies" when we were little. If you're a round ball bearing and you're taken out of that packed greased cylindrical track, and you clean out the race with turpentine, what's left are these shiny, steel marbles. Flick them with your thumb into the pool of glass marbles in a circle and try to claim as many victims as you can. Round and round the ball bearings go, where they stop, nobody knows. Round ball bearings are always good tucked underneath your tongue or bulging from underneath a cheek. Cool. Nothing beats the smooth of a steelie. Sometimes I might feel as if a marble, rolling with no control. It's not my place to decide, because the tests will decide, the microscopic attacking bugs that hide just out of human eyesight, those bacteria and viruses lodging in lungs. Rolling out of control, that's how I feel.

I tend to lose my marbles, that's why I won't play with them on the playground. Roundness rolls away, down the slant of a board, onto the cement, onto the blacktop, schoolyard pavement, into the cracks between the sidewalk, into the locked, fenced gate, just out of retrievable reach.

Where are my marbles? Are they mixed in with the iron shavings from underneath the vice, where Daddy clamped down the iron rods and sawed them by hand, leaving underneath on the cement these piles of sharp quarter-inch needles of metal? Pick them up with one of those U-shaped magnets, place them in a pile on top of a thin sheet of plywood. Wave that magnet underneath, and iron shavings dance a hula. Whee! The good thing about being a round steelie, though, is that it flows towards the path of least resistance. Downhill steelie rolls, takes a tight turn inside the ball bearing track, races towards a finish line. Round and round and round she goes, where she stops, nobody knows.

Was there really a special time that drifted in a cloud over that valley? It had been the wind in the treetops, the caressing of my hair by the breeze. It was the rubbing of bark against the tractor fender that squeaked a lively tune, wood against metal. It was the baying of the cows before they lowered their heads in the pasture to graze. It was the slaughtered cow

BRENDA NAKAMOTO

hung upside down from a tree, blood draining from its body. It was the foggy day and foggy night, a quiet chill set into the still air. It was the heavy smell of just-cut alfalfa lying in long windrows, ready to be baled. It was the hawk ornamenting the bare peach tree branches in winter. It was Mommy in the kitchen frying up chopped bacon and onions before tossing in the rice. It was Daddy at the dining table reading the *Appeal-Democrat*. It was me looking through the front dining room window wondering who I had a crush on and who I longed to have as a boyfriend.

And the foggy nights came and went, and the harvest sun rose and set, and that lonely farm faded from my consciousness, until times like this when everything I do, everything I see seems to be revolving around holding onto sight.

Daddy, throw me a rope, make it big, make it strong. You tell me today that the big, fat ropes you used to use—for tying down the double layer of peach bins onto the back of the truck when you were hauling a load of picked peaches to the grading station or for lassoing around the line of empty picking bins that you dragged from a tractor, trailing behind as if towed by a choo choo train from one end of the orchard to the other—weren't as useful as the small, thin rope you used on the farm. "What did you use rope for?" I ask you today. You are sitting now in your own bed. You look tired. Your hospital ordeal is over, but I think the brightness in your eyes has waned, your cheeks sallow.

"I don't like the breathing treatments I'm getting," you say.

I nod. I know. You have to wear a mask, and a decongestant medicine mists for fifteen minutes every six hours.

"I don't like the food here. Everything tastes bad," you say.
I know. Antibiotics kill your appetite.

"What did you use rope for?" I ask.

"For tying things together," you answer. Tying. Together. Yes, for the burlap sacks rolled up cinnamon roll style, bundled into a slipknot with a rope, connected to a short bit of wire bent into the shape of a hook and hung off the rafters in that old shed. Rope for tying the branches together in the uppermost parts of the tree. Rope for guiding the string bean runners high above my head in our garden. "Yes, you really did like the farm," you say to me, your face starting to brighten. "I'm sorry if I never told you I loved you when you were younger. I wish I could have given you a better childhood," you say.

"Oh, but I had a good childhood, a really good childhood. It was the best. Some people rather live in the city. But I enjoyed farm life." I hear my own voice explaining itself. Daddy really can't see now, can he? If he only knew.

Rope, look at how it ties us together. Rope leads from one end to the other. When it breaks, we rejoin the shredded ends with a knot. Rope—hanging from the high branches of the walnut tree and with a wooden board under my buttocks with notches cut into each side that secure the rope. I swing and swing and I swing, up and down, leaves swirling and whirling. Turn me and that swing into a tourniquet. I am squeezed tight in all that rope, a top encircled in string ready to be thrown. Let me loose, and branches flash, twisting and spinning, feet out and spiraling, feet tucked in and toes grazing the malleable earth, indenting my imprints in dust—sky and leaves horizontally blending and bleeding. I am breathless and restless. I feel the rippled and twisted fibers of rope on my fingertips, individual strands straying outward like the braid of a ponytail of a horse's mane. Push out on the rope, untangle the twists, wrap me in dizzy sensation. Rope is stringing me along.

"I'm really happy, Brenda, that you came to visit me today," you say and give me a relaxed smile. I don't think you look as yellow anymore. Your cheeks are flushed. You open your arms

BRENDA NAKAMOTO

wide; you want a hug. In your embrace, for a fraction of a moment, I think that you can really see me, just like old times, the good old days. And I can breathe, there is air, there is vision; you are the one who makes me see.

"Yes, let's talk more about rope," I say. I want more stories. "Do you think you used rope to tow the car or truck or did you use chains? Of course you used chains. Was the width of the widest rope you used about two inches in diameter? Did you rope the peach trees first and then encircle them in wire? What was that rope made of?"

YOURS ALWAYS

For you, my daddy, I write of what you can no longer see or hear. I write of things long since felt or experienced distinctly, having been covered by the veneer of dust and cobwebs of time. With blindness, you cannot distinguish clear images or walk the plowed fields of yesterday, but certainly you see the trees and orchards of the farm in your dreams. Why, the other day when I visited you, you told me you had fallen out of bed. You were showing me how you did it.

"I saw a wheelbarrow in front of me and every time I reached for it, it moved farther away. I kept trying to grab it. In fact, Bob was there and I yelled, 'Bob, get over here!' The next thing I knew I landed on the floor. I had fallen out of bed."

You are laughing, I am laughing. We are sharing a lively moment, a father and a daughter, together. My poor uncle Bob. Even in your dreams he is still getting yelled at! Some things never change. Then you add in a more serious note, a somber tone.

"I wish sometimes that I could just grab a rake or shovel so I could do some work. It would feel so good. I really enjoyed it."

You say that and I know you mean it. You think about the farm; you sometimes believe you are still on the farm. Retirement never severed your ties.

I look at you now, your diminutive figure on the bed, bundled in a white undershirt and sweatshirt and under a sheet and blanket. I see more than what's before me. I see the stars, the moon, the sun and the rain. I see tractors and backhoes and trucks. I hear mosquitoes buzzing and doves cooing and frogs croaking, blending into a contiguous, euphonious sound. And I smell peaches, fragrant fruits, soft and delicate in bins next to dusky, purple prunes. Owls hoot and rain patters on the aluminum-roofed shed. The cutting torch pops and sparks to life in a narrow blue and yellow flame, and there you

BRENDA NAKAMOTO

are, my daddy, on your knees on the cement floor in the shop pulling on a tinted safety helmet, busy at work, torching and welding tractor parts. That's what I see. You are my daddy, my strong-willed and hard-working daddy. Ever diligent and ever resolute, my daddy the peach farmer lives to today.

You are nisei, yes, persevering nisei. Japanese farmer you still are. I am sansei, ever-indebted sansei, walking in shadow.

And I am yours, always, a peach farmer's daughter.

EPILOGUE

Is a memoir ever really finished? You'll notice this one begins and ends with seasons: summer through spring. I stopped at spring because—I don't know—I always think of spring filled with birth and flowers and baby birds and blossoms. There's hope in spring, perhaps not any more or less than the other seasons, but that's the feeling I get. There's pollen in the air, birds gathering sticks, raptors migrating to nest. Hope for life never ends, I believe.

I wish Baachan and Ojiisan had written about themselves, left little bits of paper for me to discover and to hold onto, something to put my hands around. In that regard, I've written these essays to share what stories I know, these verses that somehow keep resonating in memory.

Once upon a time there was a peach farmer, and once upon a time there was his daughter.

A DAWN BREAKS

October 8, 2008

I am meeting someone who I think is my second cousin. She is the granddaughter of Mitoyo Okada, who was the older sister of my grandmother Hawayo Okada. The granddaughter and I share the same great grandparents. In the early 1900s, Hawayo moved to California while her sister, Mitoyo, stayed in Japan. It is a surreal experience, this discovery of my relatives. Tatsuya, a colleague of Shawn's in Japan, originally found this connection by asking me for the names of my grandparents and where in Japan they had been born. I had thumbed through the scant genealogical materials I had about them and given that information to Shawn, who in turn emailed it to Tatsuya. Time passed. I forgot. I didn't give it much thought. Tatsuya is the one responsible for helping us all to get to Japan. On the day before our departure from Davis, he calls and tells Shawn he found a relative of mine in Hiroshima. I am so busy packing and getting ready for the trip that I don't dwell much on it. Later, which is now, we are together in Japan, jet lagged and a bit culture shocked.

People, subways, cars, electronic billboards, people; escalators, vending machines, McDonalds, people; bullet trains, hand rails, people; flashing lights, videos, American rock and roll, people; miniskirts, boots, fishnet nylons, people; sushi, sashimi, ice cream, hot green tea, people; bicycles, rickshaws, fried noodles, broiled eel, people.

My dream this morning—Motoemon (Mitoyo's and Hawayo's father), says, "You have found home, haven't you?"

"Yes, I think so. I sense it is true."

I am told by Mitoyo's granddaughter that Mitoyo died about the same time that Hawayo died. Hawayo passed away in 1972 in Sacramento, California.

October 9, 2008

The spirits of Motoemon and Mitoyo visit with me today in
Hiroshima, Japan.

There is someone not forgotten. The black and white portraits
on the wall look down on me.

The stern and somber faces of those from before
Motoemon Okada (great grandfather)
Tora Sakurai (great grandmother)
joined in photographs by their children, Mitoyo (great aunt)
and Tatuichi (great uncle)

I confuse the names, my ears can't hear the syllables so quickly spoken.

Tora, Motoemon, and Mitoyo from my sloppy mouth blurt
out as Tore, Motoya or Mitoyemo.

I am hopelessly lost in mispronounced syllables.
Spirits of my ancestors, please guide me.

The room with the shrine and the picture of the Amida
    Buddha covering most of the wall
glowing gold, shiny, warm—candles, burning incense
an entire wall in the ten-foot-square room covered in tatami
    is devoted to prayer
in the house of Okada
on a small hill in a southeastern section of Hiroshima
ojusu clasped in my hands,

with a wooden mallet, I pound twice on the bell
sutra chanting—no one speaks, but the sounds are gushing
    in my head, remembering how the reverend used to chant
    at Sunday School

amidst the rise and curl of smoke
Someone invites me to pray in front of the altar.

Bow, put hands together within the circle of the ojusu. Yes,
yes, I remember how to do it, I can fit in, even if I was born
in America I can still share paying my respects to the Amida
Buddha as they do. I was trained. I once was so obedient.
I repeat the words.

Namu Amida Bu
Namu Amida Bu
Namu Amida Bu

She corrects. She adds the *tsu*

Namu Amida Butsu
I put my faith in Amida Buddha.

What I learned in Marysville Buddhist Church comes back to me.

My own shrine I had made from a cardboard cigar box and
orange juice cans sprinkled in crushed eggshells and spray
painted gold.

So inferior compared to what honor and reverence inhabit
this room of my second cousin's family.

Then something stirs

It is still within,
resides in my heart,
a calling from my past.
Dig deeper
I have heard those voices—them,

they were always there
these feelings, what I had thought only dreams
but they had existed

Now I know who some of them were
Great-grandparents Motoemon and Tora
and their parents
and the children
and there were others
yet even more
that I obsessed
and denied
their presence, all those morning runs when I felt them
    talking in the gusts of the north wind
of the Central Valley
Their spirits reside within me
their prayers blown across the ocean,

from Japan to the California shore

Masamichi Okada who is the great grandson of Motoemon
    Okada

tears and weeps next to me in the room.
I learn later that he had brain surgery twenty years ago.

I think he weeps because of the passing of Motoemon and Tora
Me by the altar, my second cousin at my side,

this is a reckoning
the grassy scent of tatami
shoji screen door
Shawn flashes the camera at my ancestors' photographs
    hanging on the wall
Large portraits looking at me
No hugs, no touching of hands.

Mayumi, Masamichi's sister, says to me, "We are sorry you
have travelled so far across the world to meet with us for such
a short time. We hope the next time you visit you may stay
some more."

So humble, so polite, so taking the blame for this oversight
of mine, me not allotting enough time

It is I who am sorry. I did not know it would be this way,
my family, I am home.

I bow, I hardly know what to do.
Before I leave, I try to tell the man who wept that I think I am
related to him by blood

I think that he is the husband of my second cousin, but
something in me makes me think otherwise.
It is difficult to talk with my relatives and I have to depend
on Tatsuya to interpret.

But we are pressed for time, we have to move forward.
We have to leave the house, pay respects to Motoemon and
Tora at their gravesite.
That is why we are here.
Though, I cannot leave without speaking with the weeping man.
for he deserves my attention, he is important, I sense it.
I tell him that one of Hawayo's daughters still lives in
Sacramento.

That Hawayo had five children.

I am the daughter of one; her name was Masako. She passed
away sixteen years ago.

I tell him I am grateful to have met him and I thank him for
the visit.

I bow and I leave. He bows back.

Later I learn from Shawn that he is the owner of the house.
He is now the head of the Okada family. In Japan, being the
head of the house, the head of the family name, is a very
important honor.

BRENDA NAKAMOTO

I sense a friendship, a sort of lost familiarity that suddenly
widens in my hands.

I gloat in this feeling for only a moment, because we are
running down the street.

I leave Masamich. His sister Masami and Tatsuya and I run
  to the neighborhood cemetery,
which is down the asphalt-paved mountain road
to the cement stairs that zig and zag amongst the tombstones.
A few steps down the stairs and a little community of
  gravesites opens to my view.
Tucked in between the street and some houses, not one
  square foot of space is wasted.
Oh honorable departed, let us always remember your
  presence. I bow to thee.
Far across the hillside an arching bridge spans the water.
It is over a bay or the mouth of a river.
The cemetery fills a small niche on the side of this mountain.

Shawn had said earlier as we were riding in the taxi that this
part of Hiroshima might have been far enough away from
ground zero and on the leeward side of the bomb blast to have
sustained survivors.

Down steep steps, curve to the left, down a few more steps to
reach the headstone of Motoemon.

Many headstones, packed in this community of resting souls.
Cement slabs jut upwards towards the sky.
I am sorry, we are late to meet the train that will take us from
Hiroshima to the bullet train back to Tokyo. I cannot stay long.

I put my hands together in prayer in *gassho* and bow at the
headstone where the ashes of my grandparents reside. My
second cousin points out that they are side-by-side. She shows
me the elaborate cement work of the gravestones, the Japanese
characters, the Japanese family crest, the pillars and spires,

the flowers Tatsuya had helped me purchase—white, yellow, and pink chrysanthemums—just like my mother would have.

I told Tatsuya in the taxi that he reminded me of my mother.

Yes, it had been a compliment. Everyone in the car laughed. My mother would have ensured that I bring a gift to the Okada family. She would have made sure I had flowers to place by the grave.

Tatsuya, honorable man that he is, pauses and answers a pleasant "Thank you."

Such a compliment for a proud man to be held in esteem with a woman,

and not only that, one who is my mother. He accepts graciously.

I pinch myself. Is this really happening? It feels as if I am a character in a manga.

Love lost, love found, but not really tangible. It is all happening too fast. No time, no time, but somehow it feels like there was never time.

I am reconnected to the familiar: lost and then found.

So quiet, so fleeting, so un-understandable

To Tatsuya to whom I am forever indebted

for making the call to the Nihonmachi office overseeing
    the cemeteries
Who was referred to the phone number for the Okada family.
He is told that there is only one Okada family in the
    Nihonmachi area, which is now call Hiuna, renamed after
    the end of WWII.

He makes the call; he makes the connection.

Before we leave that family for a final time, we take quick pictures at the side of the street, just above the cemetery. I face Mayumi. She is the sister of Masamichi Okada; she is the granddaughter of Mitoyo Okada, who was the older sister of Hawayo. Now she really does look like my mother, I think. Upon arrival at their house, with all of us in the taxi—and I had initially glimpsed her figure in the garage—Shawn had whispered, "That woman looks just like your mother." I had stammered. "No, can't be."

Yet now, we are saying our goodbyes and she smiles sweetly and I have this urge to wrap my arms around her and give her a good ol' American hug but I restrain myself. I bow, as I know an honorable Japanese would. I mentioned then that I was the granddaughter of Hawayo Okada and Shunjiro Sakaoka, and she looked at me for a moment, then said that I looked like a Sakaoka. She repeated it, smiling brightly. Her friend at her side commented and agreed.

And I felt again like I was home, that I had reconnected with family. That she knew Sakaokas.

I didn't know much about Sakaokas—my grandfather died before I was born—and here I was running around in life looking like one.

Suddenly I feel important, part of a bigger picture. And immediately I felt this rush of elation, with a tinge of humor because there is this thought in my head that I wasn't different, after all. I had always imagined I didn't look quite Japanese enough. I didn't have those delicate features of a refined geisha that the traditional Japanese women depicted in the movies had. My head was large, my frame stocky, my legs chunky. Now there was a reason. I was Japanese, and now I knew I was a Sakaoka.

Across from the cemetery, the ocean sprawled blue and wide, and
I wondered if we were near a feudal lord servant's home on
    the hillside
only many, many years distant
overlooking the mountain slope and bay below
At one time the samurai commanded this area, guarded their sea
an island people, a united and diligent people
building temples and shrines in honor of the great ones
who were and are still a part of us

I think I found a piece of myself in Hiroshima
a part someone who wasn't quite sure of herself
who thought she had heard voices
for all these many, many years
that rummaged only through imagination

And when suddenly she is thrust before the altar in that tiny
    house in Hiroshima,
before the headstones bearing her great grandparents' ashes
it is like they were saying hello right there, right now,
    welcoming her back
and those voices from the past whispered, yes they were
    truly spoken
they were real, they were once three-dimensional

And I wanted to speak with them some more
these voices of my ancestors
bringing me back home, again,
I've come looking and I've found you.
Hawayo and Shunjiro summoned me

A dawn breaks over the houses of the village
curved rooftops lined with red, clay tiles
Crows are cawing, greeting the sunrise

BRENDA NAKAMOTO

GLOSSARY OF JAPANESE WORDS

arigatoo	thank you
baachan	grandmother
baishakunin	a matchmaker
banzai	hurrah
bentoo	box lunch
daikon	Japanese white radish
dashi	soup stock
gassho	the act of putting hands together when praying
gobo	burdock root
goma	sesame seed
ichi	one
issei	first-generation Japanese American
kampyo	dried gourd strips
karai	salty
koko	pickled Japanese white radish
maki zushi	a sheet of nori rolled over rice & fillings
mochi	rice cakes
mochitsuki	traditional mochi-making ceremonies
namasu	vinegared seasoned raw fish
Namu Amida Butsu	total reliance upon the compassion of Buddha
nappa	vegetable greens

BRENDA NAKAMOTO

nezumi no pon pon	mouse poop
ni	two
nigiri	rice balls
nisei	second-generation Japanese American
nori	seaweed dried and processed into squares of thin and flat sheets
o sho tto	phrase used by Masa Nakamoto to give herself power, uttered like a "heave-ho"
oishii	delicious
ojiisan	grandfather
ojuzu	meditation beads
okazu	side dish served with rice
san	three
sansei	third-generation Japanese American
sashimi	sliced raw fish
shikata ga nai	it can't be helped
sushi	vinegared rice
tamashii	a spirit
tempura	deep-fried vegetables and meats
unagi	eel

ACKNOWLEDGMENTS

I owe the creation of many of the stories in this book to my late father, who always believed in me. In his younger days as a peach farmer, he inspired me to work hard at my endeavors. In his later days, even in failing health, he imparted to me the value of showing gratitude. He listened to readings of early essay drafts and offered suggestions that improved the writing.

I wish to thank my husband Shawn for having patience and supporting me while I undertook this project. My kids Toshi and Noriko put up with me in good humor, and if not for them, I may have never attempted to record my family history. I owe a huge thank you to Rae Gouirand who worked with me for numerous years in her creative nonfiction workshops and exposed me to the personal essay and memoir, and who also tested my maki zushi recipe.

I thank Kate Washington and Brad Buchanan of Roan Press for giving me this opportunity to author my first book, and I am grateful to them for having a vision to create a literary press in Sacramento that highlights area writers. I thank Kate, especially, for working with me on my edits and helping me shape the manuscript into the best that it could be, something I hope would have made my dad proud.

essays published previously in similar form

Nakamoto, Brenda. 2009. Listening to Harvest.
Blue Moon Literary & Art Review, Fall-Winter 2009, Davis CA,
4:70-74.

Nakamoto, Brenda. 2009. Okazu. *Kartika Review*,
Spring/Summer 2009, 05:39-47.

Nakamoto, Brenda. 2009. *Searching for Grandfather*.
first prize, 2008 GENEii Family History Writers Contest,
Category 2 – Family or Local History Articles, Southern
California Genealogical Society and Family Research Library,
scgsgenealogy.com/2008Geni-Winners.htm